The Hills That Beckon

By

Ray Long

Edited by Jerry Moore

ISBN: 1-4107-7244-6 (e-book)
ISBN: 1-4107-7243-8 (Paperback)

Library of Congress Control Number: 2003094943

This book is printed on acid free paper.

Printed in the United States of America
Bloomington, IN

1stBooks – rev. 08/11/03

Chapters

Dedicated to the memory of Jim and Ruby Long

Jim and Ruby Long

Acknowledgments

It will be difficult indeed to call to memory all the fine folk who have helped me over the years and have contributed to this work in a most valuable way. There are those, however, who specifically must be mentioned due to their very important contributions.

I remember visiting my good friend, Kenneth Murphy, who was head of the English department at Columbus East High School and sharing with him my intent. I will never forget his wise counsel when he said "the most difficult job you are going to have is getting the pen to move". I wish I could tell Ken just how right he was.

I would like to thank my good neighbor of many years, Janet Wolff, who, back in B. C. (before computer), was willing to type the text I had written as well as putting up with my poor grammar and spelling. And to my daughter-in-law, Maggie, who was asked to struggle through reams of hand written script producing a computer disc. She never complained, but encouraged me to press on.

A special thanks is due Dean Catlett, a long time friend of the family. When this project began, Dean was a student at Georgetown College in Georgetown, Kentucky and was kind enough to borrow for me from their library, Spencer's "History Of Kentucky Baptists". I will also mention the staff at the library of Southern Baptist Theological Seminary in Louisville. Those individuals were so helpful in providing some very old minutes of the Tates Creek Association meetings. I also want to thank the staff of the Townsend Room at the library of Eastern Kentucky University for sharing with me the "French Tipton Papers".

I would certainly be remiss if I did not mention my life long friend, Cecil Prather, who willingly shared with me information concerning his family. Thanks also go to Cecil Davis, another life long friend, whose contribution is very much appreciated. And a big thank you to a cousin, Orbin Long, whose comments on his father, Jeff, certainly added to this writing.

Jacquelyn Ross Golden of Round Hill has been such an immense help to me in my research. She not only was helpful in seeking out data at the Madison County Courthouse such as deeds, census reports and marriage bonds, but in providing me with an 1876 Beers map of Madison County. That map proved to be of great value.

Another life long friend who has been of immeasurable assistance during the development of this project is Col Neal Burnham Whittaker. Neal has no doubt grown weary over the years responding to my endless questions in regard to the Poosey area. He was especially helpful in respect to the school segment.

Someone who I owe a great debt of gratitude and appreciation is my aunt Mary Laura Long Proctor. There is no way I can properly thank her for putting up with my constant stream of questions concerning family and various other subjects.

There is a special person I wish to acknowledge: my dear wife, Sharon She is credited with naming this publication. As of this writing, Sharon and I are in our forty ninth year of marital bliss.

The following are names of some very special people who I was privileged to be able to interview and talk with individually. I am sad to say that during the time of this writing these individuals, who were so helpful in so many ways, have departed this life. They are as follows: Duke Bellamy, Paul Rhodus, Stratton Stocker, Frank Taylor, my uncle William D. Long and my aunt Roberta Long Evans. I must add that in the early days of my research, Roberta (Bert) was very helpful in supplying useful information.

Forward

At the very beginning I wish to make it clear that this venture is not intended to be a history of the Poosey area, the individual people or families who are referred to. It can best be described as a story of a family who was active in that area between the years 1791 and 1943. It also attempts to provide some information relative to other families as well as landmarks, churches, schools, country stores and a little folklore thrown in here and there.

This is an account of my branch of the Long family which began with the marriage of John D. and Winifred Tudor Long on December 1, 1791. By 1791 the Indian problem had been dealt with and for all practical purposes Madison County was free of this threat. When one thinks of the time of this marriage, it was only 16 years after Boonesborough was established. Daniel Boone was still living in the county at this time because according to various accounts he and his family moved west of the Mississippi in 1795. Pioneers began to pervade the county in the late 1780's and 1790's and establish homesteads. There is a record that Squire Boone built a cabin on Silver Creek.

Kentucky did not become a state until 1792. Therefore, John and Winny were married in Madison County, Virginia. In 1785 Virginia passed a law to create the county of Madison. In 1788 a courthouse was constructed at Milford. It seems reasonable it was at Milford where John and Winny obtained their marriage bond and license.

Milford endured for a period of ten years when the county seat was moved to Richmond. Poosey Ridge road has been in existence since probably around 1800. Because of the ferry which was in use for many years at its end across the Kentucky River into Jessamine County, it was also known as the Goggins Ferry Road as well as Hunters Ferry Road.

For years the subject of where the name Poosey was derived has been debated. Some accounts trace the name to a family named Posey who supposedly lived on the ridge at one time. Others are sure that it came from a family of Indians called "Poos" who once lived there. Most Native American authorities tell us there were no tribes actually living in this area. They only used it only for a hunting ground. If I were called upon to choose a favorite, it would have to be "Poosey is an Indian name which means "long ridge". But who really knows?

Another question I have often heard asked is, "where does Poosey Ridge begin"? In my own personal opinion, I have always felt it begins where road #876 intersects with #595 and proceeds all the way to the river. From this intersection, going north past where Whittaker's Store used to stand, past Gilead Church and the cemetery, there was a road which turned right down what was called Meet'n House Hill. This road led to what became known as Moberly Branch.

Chapter One

Moberly Branch

This stream has its beginning at a spring just over the hill from Poosey Ridge Road, on what is now the Frank Taylor property, and flows east to Silver Creek. As it was with most such streams of its kind in the area, a thoroughfare was formed to follow the stream. The thoroughfare made travel less difficult than cutting across the hills.

As travel increased along this newly formed route, it followed that homes were constructed along the way by the owners of the property. This particular branch road was named for the Moberly family who settled the area and lived there for many, many years.

Today, some of the branch roads exiting off the ridge road are still accessible and there are people still living on some of them. This is not true with Moberly Branch. Upon inspecting a recent Madison County map, it shows many of the branch roads by name and Moberly Branch is not mentioned. To someone unfamiliar with the area, they would never suspect that a road of any type ever existed there.

The truth is that at one time this was a much traveled route with houses dotting the landscape from Silver Creek almost to Poosey Ridge. Moberly Branch was never more than a wagon or sled road, but it was a road nonetheless. The actual road turned to the east just north of the Gilead cemetery. It proceeded down the hill which was known as the meeting or "meetin house hill" and ended at Silver Creek close to what was known as the Phil Moberly Place.

Moberly Branch is the area where my branch of the Longs came from. My father, Jim Long, was born in a house on what was known as Conrad Long's Hill overlooking Moberly Branch.

My grandfather, Les Long, was born in the same house as his father, Dan Long. Dan Long became owner of the property through his mother, Elizabeth Moberly, who in turn inherited it from her father, Samuel Moberly, through the settling of his estate.

Long before the Moberly family settled the Poosey area, the Silver Creek region, including a good portion of Madison County, was owned by Green Clay. Clay (1757-1828), the father of famed abolitionist and ambassador to Russia, Cassius M. Clay, came to Kentucky in 1776 in search of adventure and fortune. It did not take Clay long to recognize that success in this new frontier hinged on acquiring land. He returned to Virginia, his place of birth, to secure a license as a surveyor. Upon returning to Kentucky, he went to work clearing out tracts of land for other men who held grants in the new territory. Because of the hardships and danger involved in this job, surveyors often collected as much as half of the titled land they cleared.

It did not take Clay long to amass a sizeable amount of land. When settlers began to pour into Kentucky from Virginia and the Carolinas, many who wanted property purchased it from Green Clay.

There was a property transfer recorded at the Madison County Court House at Milford, May 7th, 1793. The county business was conducted at Milford until 1798 when the county seat was moved to Richmond. This transaction was between Green Clay and Pleasant Whitlow. The recorded transaction says in brief that Green Clay sold to Pleasant Whitlow for the sum of twenty (20) pounds current money, one hundred acres in the county of Madison and on the waters of Silver Creek. Witnesses were Andrew Bogie, Andrew Bogie Jr. and James Bogie. Will Irvine was county clerk.

This same tract of land was sold again on November 6, 1807. A brief capsule of this rather lengthy indenture says that Pleasant Whitlow and his wife Tabitha sold to Samuel Moberly, one hundred acres in the county of Madison and on the waters of Silver Creek. The amount paid was one hundred and twenty pounds. The witnesses were Joseph Holdman, Robert Porter and Humphrey Jones. The document was signed by County Clerk, Will Irvine.

Samuel Moberly purchases another tract of land from Pleasant Whitlow on November 20th, 1817. He paid sixty pounds for fifty acres. This fifty acre tract possibly joined the one hundred acres purchases in 1807. The witnesses were David Tudor and William A. Boroles. It is interesting to note that from 1793 to 1807, the one hundred acre tract of land increased in value from 20 pounds to 120 pounds. It is also interesting that Will Irvine was county clerk in 1793, 1807 and 1817.

It was mentioned earlier that the stream flowing from Poosey Ridge to Silver Creek became known as Moberly Branch. It is from Samuel Moberly, his family and descendents that it is named. Samuel Moberly came to Madison County from South Carolina in 1787. He married Ann (Anny) Tudor in 1796. They had ten children. They are as follows: John, William, Thomas, Elizabeth, Jacob, Edward, Squire, Mary, Tabitha and Benjamen. It is through Samuel's daughter, Elizabeth, that my roots are connected with Moberly Branch.

Chapter Two

Daniel I and Daniel II

Elizabeth was born around 1820 because the 1850 Madison County, Kentucky census shows her as age 30. There is further proof of not only her age but also the ages of Daniel and their son, Hayden. There are three marked graves in the Gilead Cemetery which show the following information: Elizabeth is referred to as Betty, born 1820, died 1901. I have never seen it documented, but family history suggests that Daniel's name was actually Squire Daniel. His marker shows S. Dan Long, born 1810, died 1856. Their son Hayden's marker shows Hade Long born 1836, died 1905. In various documents Hayden's name is spelled Haden or simply Hade.

The Madison County marriage records show that Anna Elizabeth Moberly married Daniel Long in November of 1834. Daniel was the son of John and Winifred Tudor Long. Winifred and Ann Tudor, who married Samuel Moberly, were the daughters of John Tudor. This fact then tells us that Daniel Long and Elizabeth Moberly were cousins.

John and Winifred (Winny) were married in Madison County on December 1, 1791. There is not a lot of information recorded about John or Daniel for that matter. John must have died sometime before 1820 because according to the 1820 and the 1830 census, Winifred is listed as the head of the household.

There was a property transfer recorded in September 1834 where Daniel Long sold 100 acres for 100 dollars to James Long. It is believed that James was Daniel's older brother since it was James who signed the marriage bond when Daniel and Elizabeth were married. This may or may not be true. This transaction reveals that the 100 acre tract of land was situated on the waters of Silver Creek. It looks as if Daniel was selling his part of the inheritance to his brother. There is no record that Daniel ever owned any more property.

It seems that Daniel, when he married Elizabeth, moved in with the Moberly family and lived there until his death. The story goes, as my father told it to me, as his father did to him and so on, that Daniel had come home around noon one day. It is not clear where he had been. He told his wife, Elizabeth, that he was going out into the side yard and lie down in the shade of a tree. She was to wake him when dinner was ready. She sent one of the children to wake him, but he could not be awakened. He died in the spring of 1856 at the age of 46, six months before the birth of his son, Daniel.

As was mentioned earlier, other than his part of the inheritance that Daniel sold to James, there is no record he owned any other property at all. It seems that when Daniel and Elizabeth were married, they began their life together in the log house belonging to Ann Moberly, Elizabeth's mother. In the 1850 census, Ann Moberly is shown living with Daniel and Elizabeth. Her age at that time was 83. Samuel Moberly died many years before and his estate went to his wife, Ann or Anny. She must have died around 1860 or 1861. A document dated December 25th, 1861, records the settling of Samuel's estate with Jacob Moberly, Elizabeth's brother, purchasing some of the land from the other heirs.

Elizabeth Long and her children are mentioned by name in this indenture. The children are named as follows: Amanda, Nancy Belle, James Howard, Daniel, Martha J., Sidney, William, Hayden, and Albert M.

Elizabeth and her children received from the estate of her father, 64 acres along with the Moberly home, which at that time I have been told was a rather large structure. A portion of this two story structure was still standing as of May, 1982. Elizabeth continued to live and raised her children here.

Most of Elizabeth's children were married and had left home by 1880. The 1880 Madison County census lists Elizabeth as head of the household with the following living with her: Nancy, daughter, age 24 (Aunt Belle Durham); Haden (Hayden), son, age 40 (Uncle

Hade); Martha King, daughter, age 32; William King, Martha's son, age 13; Dovie King, Martha's daughter, age 9; Jefferson King, Martha's son, age 7.

It is not clear exactly when Martha Jane Long was born. The 1850 census has her at age 11, which would make her date of birth 1839. The 1860 census shows her at age 16, which means she was born in 1844. The 1880 census has her age at 32, which would have her born in 1848.

Martha married Samuel King November 28th, 1865. They were the parents of three children, William (Bill), Dovie and Jefferson (Jeff). Samuel decided to go to Missouri to find work, leaving Martha and the children at home. It was rumored in the community that Samuel had deserted his wife and children, but members of this family disagree.

Ada Grizzard, a granddaughter of Samuel and Martha said that as long as Samuel was alive, Martha and the children had food, clothing and a home. It was not until after Samuel was killed in a mining accident that Martha, Bill, Dovie and Jeff went to live with Elizabeth. However, the 1880 census showed Martha's marital status as divorced.

Martha broke a hip in the fall of 1919 and died in January of 1920. She was buried in Lexington, but in the spring of 1920 a memorial service was held in her honor at the Gilead Baptist Church.

The following are the names of Daniel and Elizabeth's other children, their marriages and marriage dates are as best as can be reconstructed.

William (Will) Long, M: Elizabeth Taylor (there could be some questiion here)

Sidney (Sid) Long, M: Lucy Short

Albert Marion Long, M: Margaret Prewitt September 7, 1859, 2nd M: Mealy Warmouth.

James Howard (Uncle Doc) Long, M: Emmaline Roberts May 16th, 1864. 2nd M: Amanda Heathman 1875.

Amanda Long, M: John W. Prewitt Sept. 1, 1884.
Nancy Belle (Aunt Belle) Long, M: Joe Durham.
Hayden (Uncle Hade) Long, never married.

Daniel Long, the youngest child of Daniel and Elizabeth Long, was born in October of 1856, six months after the death of his father. Although Dan was fatherless, his brother William was 21 years old when he was born, and I am sure served as a father figure to him. Also, according to the 1860 census, Elizabeth's brother, Benjamen Moberly, was also living with them.

Dan grew into manhood living in the large log house where he was born. He, along with his mother, sisters, brothers, and other relatives, helped to work the 64 acre farm that his mother and her children had inherited in 1861.

Dan married in 1878 at the age of 22. At this point is where it becomes very confusing when trying to trace him and his parents. Dan's name was Daniel Long and his father's name was Daniel Long. So we have two Daniel Longs. This is not too unusual. Daniel Long, the father, married Elizabeth Moberly. Daniel Long, the son, also married Elizabeth Moberly. I have not been able to prove the relationship, but I am confident that Elizabeth was a cousin.

I have in my possession a copy of a marriage license and marriage certificate showing that Daniel Long and Elizabeth Moberly were married on Nov. 5th, 1878. The rites were solemnized at the residence of Rice Rose. The witnesses were Jasper C. Rose, Mary Pond, F.M. Prewitt and William Casey. The minister was John G. Pond, who beneath his name proudly wrote the word, Baptist. Other information shows that Elizabeth's father was Charles W. Moberly.

I was always told that Dan never lived anywhere except the place where he was born. The 1880 census shows him, Elizabeth and infant son, Thomas, living apart from Elizabeth, his mother.

My grandmother, Annie Long, who became part of that family in 1911, says that Dan told her that he moved away from the home place for one year. At this time, he lived on Gilead branch. The 1880 census shows Daniel, Elizabeth and son, Thomas, living with Charles Moberly, Elizabeth's father. There were three children born to Dan and Elizabeth. They are as follows: Allan B., Thomas Burton, and Nannie. Allen B. was never married. Nannie married Nathan Long. Nathan, or Nath as he was called, was the son on Sidney Long, Dan's brother. Thomas was married, but at this time it is unclear who his bride was.

I have not been able to verify the year of Elizabeth's death, but it is believed to have occurred in 1888 or 1889. Daniel remarried January 16, 1890. His bride was the former Laura Belle Hickam. Laura was 18 years old and had never been married. She was the daughter of Isaac and Nancy Jane Poynter Hickam.

Isaac Hickam is said to have come into Kentucky from Powell Valley, Tennessee during the Civil War. It is believed that he was a union sympathizer and chose not to return to his pro-confederate home after the war. He married Nancy Jane Poynter from the Madison County Community of Wallaceton. They moved into the Crow Valley area and lived the remainder of their lives there. Isaac was born October 20, 1841 and died March 10, 1918. Nancy was born February 27, 1848 and died January 8, 1937.

The marriage certificate for Daniel and Laura, dated January 16, 1890, states that they were married at the home of Isaac Hickam by Alex Ray, Justice of the Peace. Robert Long was a witness along with J. W. Hickam. When Dan took his new bride to the home of his mother on Moberly Branch, she was called upon to adjust to a rather large family living under the same roof. Besides Dan's mother, Elizabeth, there were Dan's three children from his first marriage, his two sisters, Nancy Belle and Martha Jane, Martha's three children, and Dan's brother, Hayden. There is little doubt that there were at least 12 people living at the old Moberly home, perhaps more. Martha's two children, Bill and Dovie, could have been married and gone by this time.

It was said that Laura did not have an easy time when she became Dan's wife. It seems that certain members of the family resented Laura becoming part of the family. The one who seemed to be the most vocal about Laura's presence was Nancy Belle. Nancy's resentment was to the point that she threatened to put Laura in the well. Dan took the threat seriously enough that he filled up the well. From that time on, the family had to carry their water from a spring. This incident has been put poetically:

> "Instead of slapping the hell out of Belle,
> Dan filled up the well."

Another story involved Nancy Belle, who became known as Aunt Belle Durham, and her brother Hayden, who became known as Uncle Hade Long. Hayden lived at the home of his mother along with his brother, Dan, for his lifetime. Belle also spent a considerable part of her life there along with her son, Burton. This incident occurred probably before the turn of the century:

> It seems that Belle possessed a tongue far sharper than a two edged sword. She and Hayden were engaged in some sort of dispute. She was standing in the open door at the front of the house looking back at Hayden who was either standing or sitting by the fireplace. She said something that aroused the ire of Hayden. He picked up a flat iron from the hearth and hurled it at Belle. She ducked out of the door an instant before the iron hit the door casing, leaving quite an indentation.

I visited this house, which was still standing in May of 1982, and the dent in the wood left by the iron was still clearly visible. Not only did this incident leave a mark on the wood, but also on the memories of those who witnessed it.

Chapter Three

Pa Dan and Ma Laura

Dan and his second wife, Laura, were the parents of eight children. Their first born was my grandfather, Leslie Anderson Long, born November 02, 1890. He was followed by Jeff, William McKinly, Samuel, Jenny, Charlie, Marion, and Emma. These eight children were born in a space of 22 years, the oldest, Les, born in 1890 and the youngest, Emma, born in 1912.

Dan Long died almost four years before I was born. I have always felt that I knew him personally from the stories my family, especially my father, has told. My father, Jim, and his brother, Vernon, who was only 15 months younger, spent many happy hours with their grandfather when they were growing up. They were very close to him and most of their memories of him were pleasant ones. Daniel and Laura Belle became known to their grandchildren as Pa Dan and Ma Laura.

Like most people, in that area, during this period, Dan and Laura did not often leave home. Their lives were centered around their home and family. When Dan would go to town (Richmond), he would put his wallet, or pocket book as he called it, in his suit coat pocket and secure it with a large safety pin. He was very careful with his money.

Dan and Laura did not attend church regularly. In fact, the only time they attended with any regularity was during the revivals or "Big Meetins'" as they were called. They would never miss a service for the duration. They would sit in the same place every night, the second pew from the front, next to the wall on the left.

They did not become members of the Gilead Baptist Church until 1920. Even then, they still maintained their "revival only "attendance for the most part. Mary Laura Long Proctor, their granddaughter, remembers the day they were baptized. She was about 3 years old at the time and when the minister led them out into the water, she thought he was going to drown them. Her father, Les, had to carry her to the back of the crowd so she could not see, in order to get her to settle down.

Dan believed in signs of various types. If a rooster crowed more than usual, he would say, "Laree (Laura) you'd better start gettin' ready, somebody's commin', cause that old rooster has lumbered all day."

Dan had an almost unnatural fear of fire. In extremely cold weather, he would allow only a small fire to burn in the fireplace. As my father described it, "He wouldn't have a handful of fire." He would supervise Laura as she prepared the meals. He would sit in a chair at the end of the wood range and add the wood, one stick at a time, in order to ensure that the strength of the fire was controlled.

The 64 acres that Dan and his family worked was not unlike most of the small farms in the area. They lived off the land for the most part, having a large vegetable garden, and corn that was ground into meal as well as being used for food for live stock. The cows provided plenty of milk and butter. Several hogs would be butchered when the weather got cold enough and the meat was salted down or smoked in order to preserve it.

There were many chickens which ran free, but would not venture too far away. They could always be expected to show up at feeding time.

The hens would lay their eggs in various locations, from the chicken house, if any, to the barn or out in the fields in the grass. Few were clever enough to lay the eggs where Dan could not find them. In those days eggs were used as a unit of exchange. They could be sold or traded for other goods. Dan seemed to have a never ending flow of this type of currency from his faithful hens.

Eggs could be sold or traded at any of the general stores in the area. The store that Dan used was the one closest to him on Poosey

Ridge Pike. The store was built in 1904 by Robert Long for a son-in-law, Les Cotton. It was operated from 1918 to 1919 by Millard Campbell. Cecil Broadus operated the store from 1919-1924. W.E. "Bill" Whittaker ran the store from 1924 to 1936.

Bill Whittaker had a system of giving due bills, which could be used as cash instead of paying cash for the eggs or trading them for other goods. At the end of the year, if the due bills were not used up, he would pay cash for those not redeemed. It was always a painful experience for Bill to settle Dan Long's enormous due bill account.

Twice a week Dan would get on his favorite black riding horse and with a bushel basket of eggs on each arm, he would ride from his home on Moberly branch to Bill Whittaker's store. There were several gates to be opened and closed on the way and there are people living today who saw how he accomplished this feat. He would ride up to the gate, kick it open, urge the horse through, turn the horse around, and the horse would push the gate closed with his forehead. With four bushel of eggs each week, I'm sure that Dan collected several due bills.

In 1928, Bill Whittaker decided to give a phonograph to one of his faithful customers by way of a drawing. Drawing numbers were given when goods were purchased. Neal B. Whittaker says that he was present at the drawing and his younger brother, Franklin, was asked to draw out the winning ticket. Dan Long won the phonograph and someone hauled it home for him on a sled.

Dan was a person who enjoyed a good time, and when everyone was gathered around to view the prize, a record with a lively fiddle tune was put on the turntable. Dan began to dance a jig he called "Shoot the Turkey Buzzard", which consisted of room jarring steps, along with passing his hat around and between his legs.

In the period of time that Dan Long lived, it was believed by many that certain people had the gift of healing. The people of that time are not to be confused with the faith healers of today. There was an ailment that people of that area referred to as the thrash (thrush).

12

Thrush is a condition where blisters appear on the inside of the mouth and throat. Small children are the ones most often affected by this condition. It was believed that one who never saw their father could cure the thrush by blowing into the victim's mouth. Since Dan Long's father died 6 months before he was born, people were constantly bringing their thrush stricken children to Dan. It is not known whether or not anyone ever benefited from his efforts, but he occasionally would get the disease from the child.

Dan and Laura Belle Long's grandchildren (my father, and my aunts and uncles) were very fond of them. I guess my aunt, Mary Laura Long Proctor, summed it up when she said, "When I was a child, I'd rather go there than anywhere."

Laura Belle died in the early part of 1930 and Dan died in October of that same year. In March of 1920, a little over ten years before his death, Dan Long made his last will and testament. He bequeathed all to his second wife, Laura Belle Long. Upon her death, the estate was to be divided among the 8 children of his second marriage, his and Laura Belle's children.

He was very specific about the children of his first marriage. It was stated in the will, "I devise to Nannie Long and the heirs of Thomas Burton Long, two children of mine by my first wife, nothing, as I do not desire them to have any part of my estate." His third child by his first wife, Allen B. Long was deceased by this time. He appointed Laura Belle, and his two sons (Leslie and Samuel) executors. Les and Sam did execute the will since Dan outlived Laura Belle from February to October of 1930. I have a copy of this will in my file. It is also on file at the Madison County courthouse in Richmond.

The Daniel Long family
Row 1 L-R, children of Thomas B. Long, Mrs. Thomas Long holding infant, Laura Belle Long holding infant Marion, Charlie and Jenny.
Row 2 L-R Thomas Burton Long, Leslie, Jefferson, Daniel, William McKinley and Samuel

Chapter Four

Les and Annie

As previously stated, Leslie Anderson (Les) Long, my grandfather was born November 2nd, 1890 in the same house that his father, Daniel, was born. He was the first of eight children. He was followed by Jefferson (Jeff), William McKinley (Kinley), Samuel (Sam), Jenny, Charlie, Marion, and Emma.

Les grew to manhood on the same small farm as did his father, Daniel. He received a very limited formal education and did manual labor from a very early age. He stood well over six foot, a powerful man with large hands and massive forearms. He was a gentleman in his personal attitudes toward men or women, but certainly not gentle with livestock and certain situations that raised his ire. He was not a violent man, but could become very vocal and explosive if things did not run smoothly, and more often than not, they didn't.

It is said that for every action, there is a reaction. If an action was directed toward him, boy, did Les react. Whether man or beast, fish or fowl, if they wronged Les long, they could expect retribution. The following is an example of his "get even" attitude.

The family was living at what has since been referred to as the Roy Taylor place. Les had an unusual colored hen that he was very proud of and called her his blue hen. One morning Les was shocked to find that a hawk had killed his blue hen. Determined that the hawk would no doubt return to the fresh kill, he set a steel trap on top of the dead hen. Sure enough, the hawk did return and was caught in the trap. He put on a pair of gloves to protect his hands from the hawk's beak and talons and removed it from the trap.

It was spring and still rather cool so a strong fire was burning in the fireplace. Les took the hawk into the house and held its head in the open flames until the bird was burned alive. A witness to this event was William J. Campbell, Les's father-in-law, who watched in horror as the bird went up in flames.

Later in the week, at the evening meal, when Les was not present, Jim and Vernon were talking about one of their cows that had suddenly died. Their Grandfather Campbell said, "I'm not surprised. After what your father did to that hawk, no, I'm not surprised."

Other people knew well how Les reacted to a crisis. Les' son, William D., related this account: Les and John Murphy were housing tobacco. They decided to build a framework of poles to allow the tobacco to cure outside. When the poles were secured and a large amount of tobacco had been hung, the framework collapsed. John said at once, "Now Les, don't get excited! Don't get excited!, I'll go get us a gallon of whiskey, and we'll have that tobacco hung before our faces go to sleep tonight." It is unknown whether John's suggestion kept Les' wrath in check or not.

In March of 1911, Les met Anora (Annie) Campbell. I have a letter, written to me by Annie relating the circumstances of their first meeting. She said the family was living on the property of Mr. Tom Curtis on what is known as the Curtis Pike. She had a nephew by the name of Louis Ross that she had never seen. Even though Louis was Annie's nephew, he was older than she. The family had received word that Louis was going to visit them. They were very excited about the visit since they had not seen him for several years. In Annie's own words, "He was somewhat of a rambler."

Annie's older brother, Jerry, lived in the area at that time. Jerry's wife, Lizzie, was a sister to Les' mother, Laura. Les had driven a horse and buggy to see Jerry and Lizzie. Jerry, who had also heard of Louis' visit, asked Les to drive him to see him. Again quoting from Annie's letter, "I and my sister's children had gone up in the pasture to watch for Louis. We saw the horse and buggy turn in off the pike."

Annie and the children ran to the house to tell Annie's mother that Louis was coming. She went inside and watched by the window as they drove up. She had never seen Louis, but from the description she had been given, she was sure the one driving the buggy was not Louis. Her mother said, "well, go on out and meet him". She replied, quoting from the letter, "I am not! For it's Jerry and some old thing I don't know. HA, but I sure got to know him." She never said whether Louis showed up or not.

Les and Annie met for the first time in March of 1911. They were married June 29th of the same year. Les and Annie moved in with his parents and brothers and sisters and possibly other family members such as uncles, aunts, cousins, etc.

Chapter Five

Farming on Their Own

Les and his brother Jeff were growing four acres of tobacco on the property of Conrad Long which was located across Moberly Branch to the south of Dan Long's property. Les and Annie resided the remainder of 1911 in the home of his father, then in 1912 he rented the Conrad Long property and began to farm on his own. Their first child, James Leslie Long, was born April 7, 1912. It was shortly after this that Les decided to move to Illinois.

Annie's brother James (Jim) Campbell was already living in Illinois. When Les learned of the prime Illinois farmland with its endless stretches of prairie, it was very enticing to him compared to the hilly terrain of the Poosey Ridge, Silver Creek area. Annie said that as long as they were with Jim, Les was satisfied, but after they left him, he became unhappy and moved back to Kentucky in February of 1913.

Les told me, not too many years before he died, about going to and from Illinois by train and stopping at Union Station in Indianapolis. He remembered what an enormous depot it was. He would find it hard to believe that it is no longer a depot but has been converted into a shopping mall.

After returning to Kentucky, Les rented a house and land from Mr. Cal Sowers on Moberly Branch, near his father's property. It was here that their second son, Vernon, was born September 6th, 1913. They lived at the Sower's place for a period of two years.

When Les returned to Kentucky from Illinois in 1913, he was never out of the State of Kentucky again. In fact, it is doubtful if he was ever more than fifty miles from home again. After leaving the Sower's place, they moved to the community of Red House, to the farm of Tobe Hackett.

They lived on the Hackett farm for two years and then moved into a house owned by Roy Taylor on Kelly Branch, also known as the Marg Turner Branch. This house was located between the Dry Branch Road and Poosey Ridge Road. Their third child, Mary Laura, was born here on April 18, 1917.

In 1918 and 1919, they lived in a house owned by Dee Taylor (Roy's brother) on Dry Branch. It was here that Annie's mother, Mary Campbell, died October 11, 1918. She was an invalid and had made her home with Les and Annie for several years. They bought their first farm on Dry Branch in 1920. This property later became known as the Robert Warmouth place because the Warmouth family lived here for many years.

Les decided to rent his Dry Branch property to his brother Sam, and returned to renting again from Roy Taylor. Quoting from Annie's letter, "We rented Sam our house and moved to where Roy lived before he bought the old home place on Poosey Pike." Hereafter, the family referred to this place as Roy Taylor's hill. William Daniel, their fourth child was born here on June 10, 1923. Mary Laura was named for her grandmothers, Mary Campbell and Laura Hickam. William Daniel was named for his grandfathers, William Campbell and Daniel Long. Mary Laura was always known by her first name and middle name. William Daniel was simply known as initial "D", or Dee.

Les and Annie Long and their children
L-R Roberta, William D., Mary Laura, Vernon, Jim, Annie and Les

Chapter Six

The Hollow

In December of 1924, Les Long bought the property on Moberly Branch that the family afterwards referred to as the hollow. Their daughter, Roberta was born there in February of 1926. When members of the family, the children, think of the place they called home while they were growing up, this is the place they think of. The family lived here from January 1925 until late 1936.

This house was located at the foot of the hill almost directly behind Gilead Church. It was a two story log structure with a massive stone chimney on the east side.

When Les bought the property in 1924, it was purchased from the heirs of S.B. Moberly. The house and land had been Moberly property for many years. Les continued to own the property after he moved to Poosey Ridge Road in the fall of 1936. Several of Les' children moved into this house after they were married.

My parents and I lived here on two occasions. I have many memories surrounding this house. It was here that my mother, Ruby, encountered the skunk. It was during the spring of 1942. I had not felt well that day and did not go to school. I began to feel better in the afternoon and was sitting on the back door steps eating chocolate pudding and watching my pup, "Snip," play. My grandfather had given me the mixed breed pup which was about three months old at the time. Snip was approximately thirty feet from where I was sitting when a strange thing happened.

Around the corner of the house came, what I thought at first glance to be my grandfather's black and white cat, but then realized, to my horror, was a skunk. And even more horrifying, the skunk attacked my pup! The cries of the terror stricken puppy combined with my own screaming and yelling brought my mother to the back door.

She surveyed the crisis and sprang into action. The only weapon available at this time was a mop leaning against the house. She grabbed the mop and with the form and accuracy of a professional golfer, knocked the skunk free of the puppy. She then did something that to this day, I find hard to believe. She somehow was able to pin the skunk to the ground by the neck with the mop head until it choked to death.

It took several minutes to accomplish all of this, and as one might guess, the skunk was not completely defenseless. While Mom was applying the pressure with the mop, the skunk was applying pressure of its own. Although she was being sprayed with the skunk's not to pleasant perfume, she did not forsake her post, but stayed to the bitter, and I do mean bitter, end. When Dad came home, it was his unpleasant duty to bury the skunk. Mom had to burn her clothes. The odor seemed to hang in the air for several days to remind us of those unhappy moments.

I have often thought of this incident because skunks are normally very shy animals who as a rule, would never attack. Because they usually only defend themselves, I have concluded that the skunk could have been rabid. Rabies is common among skunks.

It was also during this time period that Dan's hat went up in flames. Dan, whose real name was Charles Daniel, was the son of Jeff and Belle Smith Long. Dan's mother died when he was quite young and he became a frequent visitor to his uncle, Les Long. Dan was always welcome as he was good natured and had a keen sense of humor.

I recall putting his good nature to the test when I was a small child. It was probably around 1939. The weather was cool and a strong fire was burning in the fireplace. Dan was on his way to visit his Uncle Les when he decided to stop at our house for a visit. He was wearing an old felt hat, which had seen better days, and he removed it when he sat down. Probably more mischievous than curious, I picked up the hat and put it on my head. Dan grinned and said,

"Ray! do you know that hat's got lice in it?" I tore the hat from my head and threw it into the blazing fire where it was consumed in an instant. He did not get upset, but thought the whole thing to be funny. Needless to say, my parents did not think it was funny at all. I have no idea if they ever replaced that hat.

From the time he was a small boy Dan would work for his Uncle Les, doing whatever needed to be done. He was a good worker and soon gained a reputation that led to additional work throughout the community. Being a hard worker, Dan appreciated that quality in others.

There was a Poosey Ridge resident who had the reputation of being one of the hardest working men in the area. No one would dispute the fact that this man was a very hard worker. The man was hanging tobacco and fell out of the barn and died as a result. A day or so later, a group of men including Dan were gathered at Whittaker's store discussing the demise of the unfortunate gentleman. Dan said, "Well! I don't know where he went...but where ever it was, he'll make 'em a good hand."

We get a picture of Dan, as a family man, from a memory shared by his daughter, Frances. She said that when Dan's children were small, he would sit with them on his lap in a rocking chair and sing the old English ballad, "Barbra Allen."

I saw Dan last at my grandfather's (Les Long) funeral in April of 1973. One year later, April 1974, Dan, his wife, Mary Annise, and their daughter Barbara were the victims of a tornado that left a total of seven people dead in Madison County.

After I became an adult, I had no contact with Dan, except for the brief encounter in 1973. But he was a part of my childhood and part of my family and I cherish my memories of him.

It was at this log house on Moberly Branch years earlier that Vernon used the front door step to kill a snake. Roberta, who became known as "Bert", related this story. She said that when she was a

23

small child, she and her brother, Vernon, were going up Moberly Branch toward home. She was riding behind Vernon on a horse they called "Old Sorghum." They were riding bare back with only a work bridle on Sorghum.

Vernon spied a rather large non-poisonous snake, and having no fear of the reptile, slid off the horse and grasped it with one hand just behind the head. The snake then coiled itself around Vernon's arm. Bert was observing all this from the back of the horse, and the horse had by this time become quite excited, a horse being instinctively afraid of snakes.

Vernon somehow managed to get back upon the horse, the snake still wrapped in a great coil around his arm. Quite a ruckus ensued then with Vernon shouting at the horse, trying to get it under control, and Bert yelling at the top of her voice for fear of the snake as well as the excited horse.

When Vernon got the horse headed in the right direction, Bert said she had one of the wildest rides of her life. She was afraid to hold on to Vernon because of the snake and afraid not to for fear of falling off.

Bert said that her mother, who was home at the time, could hear the hoof beats of the running horse and her screams of terror. When Vernon got the horse stopped in front of the house, his mother threatened him within an inch of his life and ordered him to dispose of the snake.

There was a large flat rock in front of the log structure that was used as a door stop. Vernon killed the snake on that rock. The rock could still be seen at the time of this writing.

Chapter Seven

A Journey Down Moberly Branch

A frequent visitor to the house in the hollow was William Jasper Campbell, the father of Annie Long. He was referred to by the children as Pa Campbell. The children of Les and Annie did not seem to have the close relationship with their Grandfather Campbell that they did with their grandfather Long (Pa Dan).

While Dan Long was a good natured, fun loving playful person, William J. was a sober, no nonsense and sometimes gruff individual. He somehow acquired the nickname of the Judge. In a photograph of him taken around 1925, he has a long white beard and exemplifies sternness personified.

I am not sure exactly what kind of domestic life he and his wife, Mary, had. They seemed to live apart even before her death.

William J. Campbell, son of Jeremiah and Louise Northern Campbell was born in Knox County, Kentucky on August 17, 1852. Some accounts say Tennessee. His wife, Mary L. Hutchens, daughter of Thomas and Elizabeth Steel Hutchens, was born in Estill County, Kentucky on December 8, 1856. The Campbell family did not seem to live any length of time in any one place.

A few years after Les and Annie were married, Mary became totally disabled. She was paralyzed from the neck down with arthritis. She moved in with Les and Annie and lived with them until her death on October 11, 1918. I have been told that Les and Mary were very fond of each other. From the time that Mary became ill, William J. did not attempt to have a home of his own but would live with his children who were all married and had families of their own. He became a familiar figure in the Poosey–Silver Creek area until his death February 27, 1929.

Today if one walks from Silver Creek up Moberly Branch toward Poosey Ridge, no doubt one could see the remains of one former dwelling house...that of Dan long. But in the time that William Campbell walked this area, he would pass the house of Phil Moberly at the mouth of Moberly Branch at Silver Creek, and the house of James Howard (Uncle Doc) Long, and then the homes of Sid Moberly, Dave Lewis, and the Portwood home followed by a home owned by Cal Sowers, but not his residence. And then of course the Dan Long property and an old log structure that was also Moberly property that Sam Long lived in at one time. This was known by my family as Sam's old house.

The last house on the branch before getting to Poosey Ridge was the Les Long property that was known as the hollow. The only houses that I can personally remember are the hollow where we lived, Sam's old house and the Dan Long house.

The house known at that time as the Phil Moberly place, at the mouth of Moberly branch on Silver Creek, is still standing today and I'm sure it is still a residence. I'm sure that there is much that could be said concerning all of the homes that were located along the branch in that bygone era, but there are two specifically that deserve to be mentioned. Not the homes themselves but regarding the people who lived there. Dave Lewis, a black man, lived in one of these houses with his family. According to the 1880 Madison County census his family consisted of him, along with his father and mother. From all reports, Dave was a good man, well liked and respected by all who knew him. I have heard my father say that Dave had the ability to fashion a watering trough from a log that would not leak, a feat that few men could duplicate. The home that my family referred to as Sam's old house was also home to other members of my family. After Sam purchased the home of his father, Mary Laura and Luther Proctor lived there for a year. Vernon and Pauline Long moved there for a while and their first child, Martha Frances, was born there.

Chapter Eight

The Phelps Light

In that not so long ago time, people seemed to accept an apparition matter of factly. There is a tale that I will share called simply, The Phelps Light.

The legend of the Phelps light has persisted for many, many years in the Poosey area. Like most legends, the story has had a tendency to grow with the passing of time.

The story goes that a man named Phelps was walking from Silver Creek toward the ridge road one cold stormy night carrying a lantern, although some accounts say a torch. The man became exhausted, fell to the ground and died. Some accounts say he froze to death.

From that time on residents of the area have told stories of seeing a light bobbing along the same path Mr. Phelps took, especially, on cold, dark, stormy nights. The light, to my knowledge, has never been explained other than the possible ghost of Mr. Phelps. If it were explained, I'm sure it would ruin a perfectly good story.

Members of my family, my father included, declare that they have seen this light. They trace Mr. Phelps' route a bit more thoroughly than others. They claim he was walking parallel with Moberly Branch toward Poosey Ridge when disaster struck. A large flat rock on Sowers Hill across the branch from the former Dan Long property is pin-pointed as the place where Phelps met his demise. It seems that this story has been confined primarily to the Gilead, Moberly Branch area, although some may dispute this.

The story has existed for generations in my family. On a trip to Poosey in October of 1985, I talked to some life long residents about the Phelps light. They replied as follows:

Frank Taylor: He said that he and Burdette Agee were in the Moberly Branch area late one evening about 1960. They saw a light moving along that they could not explain. He said that he has no idea what it was. He had not seen it before nor has he seen it since.

Duke Bellamy: He said that he had heard of it all of his life but had never seen it.

Paul Rhodus: He said that he had never seen it, but his father, James Rhodus, had seen it many times.

In 1991, I visited Cecil Davis who grew up in this area and now lives in Madison, Indiana. Cecil acknowledges seeing this light many times. At one time, the Davis family lived on Hendren's Ridge overlooking Moberly Branch. He said that on cool damp nights, he would see the light moving along and at one point it would seem to stop. There were times when the light remained in one spot for a while and he and his brother, J.W., would get on horse back and hurry to that spot hoping to identify it. However, when they reached the approximate location, the light would vanish.

The Phelps light is a little bit of Poosey Ridge folklore that we like to hold on to. Whether it is mystery or myth, fact or fiction, let each person decide for himself what he would like the Phelps light to be.

Chapter Nine

Jim and Vernon

Jim and Vernon grew to young manhood while living in the hollow. Jim was twelve when the family moved there and Vernon was seventeen months his junior. It is here that their memories are most vivid, associated with their "growing up" experience.

Their days, when not in school, were filled with farm labor. But all was not work. There was play such as rabbit hunting during the day and hunting nocturnal animals at night, such as opossum (possum) and Raccoon (coon). They were not expected to work on Sunday, except for feeding livestock and milking cows.

This was the period when the relationship with their paternal grandparents, Dan and Laura Long was solidified due to the proximity of the two residences. During this period in the mid twenties, William McKinly (Kinly), Charlie, Marion, and Emma were still living at home and they became more like family. Sam and his family also lived nearby. There was much visiting between the families, especially on the weekends.

Jim and Vernon slept upstairs in the old log house and had it pretty much to themselves, except when visited by their grandfather Campbell. When he visited, he also slept upstairs with the boys who were admonished to be quiet so their grandfather's slumber would not be disturbed.

There were numerous rock fences which crisscrossed the farm in the hollow. These fences were, no doubt, laid by the first people who settled this area. They were immigrants or direct descendants of immigrants from England and Scotland, since this same type of stone fence has been found in the British Isles for centuries. These rock fences bring to mind an adventure that Jim and Vernon had when they encountered such a fence.

Dan Long's daughter, Jenny, was married to Robert Oliver. Robert, a good devout man, was quite a craftsman and Les hired him to make a sled. This was a farm sled, a heavy duty type common to the area, which was normally pulled by a team of horses or mules. However, when there was snow on the ground, the sled could be pulled by two people without too much effort. When the sled was finished and a light snow had fallen, Les sent Jim and Vernon to pull the sled home.

I'm not sure which route they took in getting home, but they arrived at the top of the hill overlooking the house and barn. After towing the sled all this distance, the boys decided to ride the remainder of the trek. After getting the heavy sled started, they each jumped on for the final leg of the trip.

The weight of the sled plus the extra weight of their bodies combined with the new fallen snow caused the speed of the sled to increase rapidly. The boys were so anxious to ride the sled downhill that it didn't occur to them as to how they were going to stop. This was not a problem, however, as the sled hit a rock fence breaking a cross beam, and rendering the sled useless and in need of repair. Needless to say, Les took a dim view of the entire incident.

When Jim and Vernon reached their mid to late teens, they, (as they referred to it), "Got big enough to run around". Their running around usually consisted of riding horseback to one of the many revivals (Big Meetings) at Gilead, Corinth, Salem or Beech Grove. The teenage girls could always be expected to be at these revivals, so it followed that the young men could be found there too.

Even though the automobile had become quite common by the late twenties and early thirties, very few young men in the Poosey, Silver Creek area owned an auto. Horses were still the major mode of transportation for most young men in this area. Jim had a black horse that he called "Old Dud". It was an easy gaited saddle horse. In talking to Vernon not too long ago, he said that riding "Old Dud" was like sitting in a rocking chair.

The revival meetings were usually well attended. The roads were crowded with pedestrians, horses, buggies and a few autos, mostly model-T Fords. Many of the young men who went never intended to go inside. When energetic young men get together and have time to kill waiting for the services to be over so they can walk the girls home, their time is sometimes used in plotting mischief.

The law regarding disrupting worship was taken very seriously in that period, and some young men found themselves in trouble for what they considered to be a harmless prank. Some of the pranks that I have been told about consisted of throwing a goose through an open window, and pushing a goat through the front door of the church.

These meetings were usually held during the summer and the windows had no screens. There is a story about a man who had fallen asleep by an open window during the sermon. Two fellows, observing him from the outside, attempted to pull him through he window. The clamor that followed with the man yelling and kicking did, in fact, disturb worship.

Jim and Vernon were charged with disturbing worship one time. Jim said he didn't think they disturbed worship because a few of the fellows were just horse racing on the road in front of the Church. This incident occurred in Garrad County on Buckeye Pike in front of the Methodist Church. Their father was called upon to pay the fine, which he did. The boys were threatened within an inch of their lives and were told that they were to pay back the money.

The boys hit upon a scheme. They promised their father if he would buy an automobile, they would help him pay for it. Les took them up on the offer and purchased a two or three year old Essex in 1928. Sam also bought a Chevrolet about this same time. They built a two car garage across the road from the Ali Williams property at the head of Moberly Branch road. Les and Sam lived on the Branch at this time, and it would be extremely difficult for an auto to negotiate those hills and hollows.

During this "running around" period, Jim and Vernon developed a reputation as singers. They did not perform before an audience or for the benefit of others, but they would lift their voices in song as they traveled late at night from one point to another. While talking with Leman Oliver several years ago, he mentioned Jim and Vernon's singing. He said, "They would make these hollows ring".

In a visit to Poosey Ridge in October of 1985, I was privileged to talk to Paul Rhodus. He told me that as a boy, he would lay in his front yard on warm summer nights and listen to Jim and Vernon as they rode up Trace Branch toward Poosey Ridge Road. They had been to a revival at Corinth Christian Church on Silver Creek. They sang as they rode, not one of the hymns they had just heard, but a song called "Columbus Stockade Blues".

Jim turned 18 in April of 1930 and Vernon became 17 in September of the same year. The years1930 and 1931 were no doubt the peak years for their running around experience. It was at that time that they, as it was called, began to talk to the girls.

Jim Long riding "Old Dud"

Chapter Ten

Jim and Ruby

Jim began to get interested in a girl by the name of Ruby Anglin. Ruby attended the Gilead Baptist Church on a regular basis, becoming a member in 1928. Since the Long Family also attended Gilead, Jim and Ruby just sort of gravitated toward one another.

Ruby was the daughter of Denny and Fannie Ward Anglin. Fannie was short for Frances Elizabeth. They were natives of Rockcastle and Laurel Counties respectively, he being born in April of 1887 and she in August of 1888. He was the son of John and Elsie Garrett Anglin and she the daughter of William T. and Eliza Stoaks Ward. Denny and Fannie were married in 1908 and were the parents of five children: Clarence, Ruby, Vernon, who died at any early age, Ruth and Clifford. Denny was a farmer for most of his life. He was a hard worker and a capable man, but never seemed to find the right location or situation to settle down. Most of Denny and Fannie's married life can best be described as transitory. Their travels were patterned, from Kentucky to Indiana. They moved to Ohio once, but mainly back and forth between Kentucky and Indiana.

When I was a small child, Ruby told me of one such sojourn the family had taken from Indiana to Kentucky. A few years before her death, I asked her to write down the details of this trip for me and the following is a paraphrase of her writing.

"We moved from the Community of Wallaceton, Kentucky to Paris Crossing, Indiana in January of 1920. In April 1921, the decision was made to move back to Madison County, Kentucky. We moved in a covered wagon, Mom, Dad, Ruth and I. Ruth was six months old. Clarence had left a day or two before with the man who took our furniture by truck.

We drove two horses, "Old Bill", a little bay horse, and "Barney", a big roan. Bill would get scared each time he saw a train or interurban car (a single train car, usually electric, used to travel from one urban area to another).

We crossed the Ohio River on a ferry at Madison, Indiana. This was great fun for me since I was only nine years old. As Daddy would drive, he would eat kraut from a large jar setting on the floor of the wagon beside him. There were times when I would ride with him on the driver's seat. On one occasion, when I was riding with him, I put my foot in his jar of kraut.

We stayed the first night, which was Sunday, in Bedford, Kentucky. We put the horses in a livery stable and stayed in a hotel. We started early the next morning and it was dark by the time we reached Bagdad, Kentucky, where we spent the night with friends. We had a lantern lit in the wagon while Dad was trying to find the livery stable. The lantern caught fire and Mom threw it into the street where it was broken.

The following night, we reached Nicholasville, where we stayed at Arch Whitaker's hotel. The next day, we crossed the Kentucky River at the end of Poosey Ridge and arrived at our new home late Wednesday evening. We had our buggy tied to the back of the wagon. We had plenty of food and stayed there until fall."

Denny's transit lifestyle continued as he moved to White Lick Creek in Garrad County for one year. His brother, Noah, who lived in Indianapolis, owned a small farm at Cartersville. Denny moved there and stayed approximately three years. He moved back to Indianapolis, Indiana in late 1925 or early 1926 only to move to Franklin, Ohio, in April of 1926. In October of 1926, the Anglin family moved back to a Kentucky farm in the Poosey area known as Daily Ridge. Even though the family lived in various locations, they stayed in the Poosey area for several years.

It was some time after this that Jim and Ruby began to notice each other. By 1931 and 1932, things began to get serious. Jim's sister, Mary Laura, married Luther Proctor in February of 1932, a marriage that is securely intact as of this writing. Vernon married Luther's sister, Pauline Proctor. The Les Long household was just over the hill from where the Anglins lived on Daily Ridge. Denny was an old fashioned type father who would not allow his daughter to date. However, love always finds a way and Jim and Ruby were determined to further their relationship in spite of Denny's objections.

There was a large rock under a maple tree some distance from the Anglin residence. After her family was asleep, Ruby would slip out of the house to meet Jim at the rock. They, as Ruby put it, would use the rock for a post office. They each would put letters under the rock to be picked up by the other unobserved. I have in my possession one of these letters written by Jim in the spring of 1932. Ruby told Jim that if her Dad caught her, she would roll the rock down the hill and he would know what had happened.

In the first part of June, 1932, Jim and Ruby began to make plans for a wedding. How this was to be accomplished without raising Denny's suspicions was a matter of concern. Fannie, Ruby's mother, was not a problem, as their intentions had been divulged to her. How Ruby was to leave the house and go to Richmond, the county seat, without Denny being the wiser was the challenge.

June 18, 1932 was chosen as the fateful day. The plan of deception was designed in the following manner: Ruby had asked her cousin, Hazel Campbell, who was a few years younger than she, to accompany her to Richmond for a day's shopping. Hazel was not aware that she was to be part of this great deception. Hazel was the daughter of Horace and Kate Campbell. Kate was Fannie Anglin's sister. Ruby asked her father if she, along with Hazel, could go to Richmond with Mr. and Mrs. Long (Les and Annie) for the day. Denny saw no harm in this. After all, he had known Mr. and Mrs.

Long for some time and they were neighbors. One thing Ruby failed to tell her father was the Long's son, Jim, would be going as well.

On June 18, 1932, James L. Long and Ruby M. Anglin were married at the First Baptist Church in Richmond, Kentucky. The Rev. Clyde Breland performed the ceremony. The witnesses were Leslie A. and Annie Campbell Long. They too were part of the deception. The newlyweds knew that they would have to face the music sometime, so they decided to tell Denny together when they returned from Richmond. They expected Denny to rant and rave and I am sure he did not disappoint them.

Jim and Ruby had made no plans as to where they were going to live. Under the circumstances, they were taking things one step at a time. While Denny was still fuming, Jim started down the hill toward the home of his parents, leaving his new bride with hers. As he was going down the hill, Denny called to him, "Come on back, Jim, you can stay here." Jim and Ruby lived with her parents on Daily Ridge until January, 1933.

Chapter Eleven

A New Beginning

The two families then moved to Poosey Ridge Road to the Lem Whitaker property, the present Stratton Stocker property. In January, 1934, Jim and Ruby moved out on their own to the property of Lewis Lamb on Taylor's Fork Creek. Lewis shared his home with Mr. and Mrs. Frank Srewsberry. Lewis remained a bachelor his entire life. He was one of the first in the area to purchase a radio. He would invite neighbors to his home to listen to this new marvel of entertainment. He remarked to Jim that when he turned the radio on, the fellow already had his fiddle under his chin ready to play.

Lewis was a good farmer and an excellent business man. In the days before the huge lending institutions, there were certain men in the community who could and would lend money. Lewis was one of these. A promissory note was usually signed, but sometimes a hand shake was good enough. When Les Long purchased the property from Ali Williams on Poosey Ridge Road, the money was furnished by Lewis Lamb. I knew this man personally and saw him last in the summer of 1953 in Richmond, where I introduced him to my fiance', Sharon Kay Tilley.

Jim and Ruby lived on Taylor's Fork Creek until November, 1935. It was there that their son Ray, author of this narrative, was born. Dr. Russell Pope was the attending physician. Jim and Ruby cultivated new friendships during this time. Among them were Roy and Zelma Smith and Lawrence and Mattie Richardson.

In November of 1935, Jim, Ruby and son moved into the house where Jim was born, the Conrad Long property. My earliest memories begin at this location, even though they are fleeting, shadowy images. I remember a black cow with a white face and a sorrel horse called "Old Choc".

38

It was in October of 1936 that Les purchased 13 3/4 acres from Ali and Amanda Williams, across from the Gilead Cemetery on Poosey Ridge Road. This had been known as the Mark Tudor Property for many years. Les continued to own the property on Moberly Branch, known as the hollow. In late 1936 or early 1937, the Jim Long family moved to the hollow.

My memories of the first two years spent in the hollow are clear. It is during this period that I began to establish relationships with other family members such as aunts, uncles, cousins, etc. Since Les and Annie moved up on the Ridge Road, it evolved into the gathering place for the family on Sunday. Those normally in attendance were Mary Laura and Luther Proctor with their two children, Vernon J. and Orline, Vernon and Pauline with their children, Martha Frances, Betty Jean and Marvin, and of course, Jim, Ruby and their son Ray. William D. and Roberta were not yet married.

There was much laughter at these gatherings and lots of singing. There was a pump organ that Roberta played and a guitar or two around as Vernon and Roberta both played the guitar. Jim even played the guitar at one time, but abandoned that pursuit shortly after he and Ruby were married.

Roberta and William D. did marry in the early 1940's. She to James Agee and he to Ethel Neeley. They had one child each. The Agee's, a little girl named Patricia Ann that we called Trish, and D. and Ethel a boy, William Leslie who became known as Billy.

Chapter Twelve

Les' Brothers and Sisters

Samuel (Sam) Long, Les' brother purchased his father's property on Moberly Branch after Dan's death in 1930. Sam and his wife, the former Leoma Thomas, and their three daughters, Louise, Clyde and Jewel Dean, became familiar figures as they were often in our home as we were in theirs. Of Les' brothers and sisters, I was probably closer to Sam than any of the others. This was due of course to the proximity of our dwellings.

Although I saw Dan often, I only saw his father, Jeff (Les' brother) occasionally. Jeff was the father of several children. Jeff's first wife was Belle Smith. Their children were Laura Belle, Dora Mae, Thomas and Charles Daniel (Dan).

After Belle's death, Jeff married Stella Masters. The fruits of this marriage are as follows, but not in chronological order: Della, Geneva, Fannie Moore, Elsie, Opal, Jereal Dean, Russell Lee, Orbin, one set of twins, (one died in infancy), Marie, Milton Way, Oma and Alma, (both died at an early age). I apologize if there are errors or omissions in the above mentioned list of names.

Jeff became known as a cunning live stock trader, especially when it came to horses and mules. The following accounts attest to his prowess as a trader.

Hanson Moberly was driving a team of mules in the Crow Valley area. Now these were pretty good mules, but both of them were practically deaf. He saw Jeff Long, accompanied by his son Dan, driving a team of mules hitched to a wagon.

Moberly, who fancied himself quite a horse and mule trader, saw an opportunity to unload his hard of hearing mules. When Jeff was asked if he would be interested in trading teams, he said, "Yeah, I'll trade, but I'll have to see your team work".

While Jeff unhitched his team and hitched Moberly's team to his wagon, Moberly stood nearby whittling a sharp point on a stick. He knew when Jeff spoke to the team that they couldn't hear, so he jabbed the lead mule in the side at an angle where Jeff couldn't see.

Jeff was so impressed with the way the team responded that he agreed to trade teams. Moberly went on his way, pleased with himself in the manner in which he had trimmed Jeff, until he discovered that the team he had traded for was about blind.

Moberly did not tell this story for several years after the trade. This story was told to me by Orbin Long, Jeff's son.

One of the traditions of Southern towns that has been lost is court day. Some small towns still boast of having court day, but it has been reduced to nothing more than a flea market. Richmond's court day was held on the first Monday of each month.

This was an important event in the later part of the nineteenth century and the early 1900's. In fact, there was still considerable activity as late as the 1930's. This was the day court was in session at the court house, and those who had anything to sell or trade would bring them to unload.

Horse and mule trading was the main part of the activity, but dogs, guns and pocket knives were other sought after commodities. Most of the horse and mule trading was done on First Street, on the east side of the court house between Main and Irvine Streets. It is not clear exactly when this trade took place, but Wilburt Teater witnessed this transaction and related it to Jim Long:

He said that Jeff Long had traded for a horse that he knew absolutely nothing about. He then set about to sell or trade the horse to someone else. He began to talk to a man who was looking for a horse to drive in his buggy. When he asked Jeff if the horse would drive, Jeff replied, "Yes sir, he is a good driving hoss."

They agreed to a trade and the man proceeded to hitch his good driving hoss to the buggy. Jeff very quickly disappeared into the crowd. Wilburt, who was observing all of this, said that when the man spoke to the horse, he took off like a shot. The last time he saw man, horse and buggy was when they turned the corner from First on to Water Street on two wheels with the man standing in the buggy trying to control the horse.

William McKinley, no doubt named for the president of the same name who was elected in 1896, was the third child born to Dan and Laura Long. Called Kinley or Mac by his family, I saw him from time to time when he visited his brother Les when Les lived on Poosey Ridge Pike. One clear memory I have of Kinley is of him sitting in the living room of Les' home playing the guitar and singing, "One Day When I Was Lost, He Died Up on the Cross". Kinley's first marriage, to Cathrine Chastien produced three children. They are as follows: Mary Frances, Hattie Lee and Annie. His son Lewis Ray was born to his second wife, Delia Lunsford.

Charlie and his wife, Eula Masters, were the parents of two children, James Robert and Anna Belle. Jenny married Robert Oliver, a widower who had children. The children of Robert and Jenny were Zora, Lonzie, James Marvin, Viola, Elwood, and Edna.

The two younger children of Dan and Laura Bell, Marion and Emma, had no children. I have been told that in the year 1912, the year Emma was born, there was a family by the name of Applegate that lived across the hollow from the Dan Long home. The Applegates lived in the old log house we called "Sam's old house". Mrs. Applegates's first name was Emma. When Laura's last child, was born, she named her Emma because of the help Mrs. Applegate was to her during this period.

Marion was the youngest son, and Charlie was a few years his senior. As I recall, Marion was a good natured, but quiet individual. He was very quiet and unassuming compared to Charlie. Charlie was a happy-go-lucky, life of the party type of fellow who never saw a stranger. He was quick with a joke and could sum up a situation in a comical fashion. The following two accounts are examples of Charlie's ability to deal with a crisis in various areas.

Paul Rhodus and Vernon Long were standing at the corner of First and Main Street in Richmond when Charlie, Vernon Long's uncle came along and joined in the conversation.
Charlie, who was between wives at the time, said to Vernon, "Vernon! You don't know where a body could pick up an old plug woman to make a crop with, do you?"

Paul Rhodus personally told me this story in October of 1985.

William D. Long and his uncle, Charlie, were driving a team and wagon from the Dry Branch area to William D's home on Poosey Ridge Road. It was getting late in the day and "D", as he was called, urged the team into a trot.

The single trees began to move in a see-saw motion, which disturbed a bay horse named Frank. This horse, which already had developed a reputation for having a mean streak, began to kick at the traces.

"D", who was driving and very familiar with Frank's tactics, pulled the team into a fence near Mrs. Pearl Taylor's barn. This action caused Frank to fall across the wagon tongue where he found himself on his back and unable to get up on his own.

When "D" and Charlie removed themselves from the wagon to survey the situation, Charlie said, "D"! "You know what we ought to do?"

"What?" replied "D".

"We ought to go to the store, get a five gallon can of gas, pour it all over that S.O.B. and burn him up".

Chapter Thirteen

Family, Friends and Neighbors

Roberta, Les and Annie's daughter, was born February 24, 1926. She was near the age of her cousins: Louise, Clyde and Jewel Dean, the daughters of Sam and Omi (Leoma). Bert, as she became known, lived in the big log house in the hollow until she was ten years old. She developed a fast friendship with her cousins who lived just down Moberly Branch a short distance. The relationship has endured until this present time.

As children, the four girls spent a great deal of time together. Children have always been able to express themselves in play in one way or another. Children made do with what they had in the years before television, electronic games and other devices which entertain today's children. Many would resort to the world of make-believe. So it was with Roberta, and her three first cousins, Louise, Clyde and Jewel Dean Long. The following recollection was shared by Roberta. It was one of many pleasant memories she had with her cousins.

The church was the social center of the community, so it follows that those events were often imitated in children's play. Roberta (Bert) was visiting the three sisters, and they decided to play church in the barn. Louise was the preacher and would sit quietly with legs crossed during the preliminaries on the make-believe pulpit. Jewel Dean was the organist using a grate (a fire-place insert for coal) as an organ. At times, Louise would not be satisfied with the way Jewel Dean was playing and would say, "Jewel Dean! If you're going to play that organ, play it and quit handling it like it's nasty".

With Louise preaching, Jewel Dean playing the organ and Bert leading the singing, Clyde was the only one left in the congregation. After Louise delivered a soul stirring sermon, Clyde would become convicted of sin and rush to the alter to agonize and ask forgiveness. After Clyde was received by the church, all four girls would mount a mule, "Old Sid", that was hitched in the drive-way of the barn, and ride him bareback in back of the barn to a sweet fern patch which was their baptismal pool. Louise would lead the candidate into the baptismal sweet fern patch holding a tobacco stick in one hand to gauge the depth as they walked. After a verse of "Shall we gather at the River", Clyde was buried in the vegetation and raised to newness of life.

During our first tenure in the hollow, 1937-1939, I became aware of not only family, but also neighbors who became important. Up the hill from the hollow on Daily Ridge, lived Lewis and Willie Moore Ward. They lived for a while in the same house where my Grandfather Anglin had lived. My family was very close to the Wards. In fact, my mother considered Willie Moore to be her best friend. They became acquainted when my mother's family began to attend Gilead Church in 1925.

Willie Moore's mother died when she was quite young. She and her siblings continued to live with their father, Willie Lee Elswick, who never remarried. I have heard my mother speak often of going home, after church on Sunday, with "Pug" (Willie Moore) as she was called. The house would be spotless and Mr. Elswick would have a delicious meal prepared.

My mother always had a tremendous amount of respect for Mr. Elswick who, after the death of his wife, remained totally devoted to his children. Mrs. Elswick was the former Bessie Moberly. Her parents were Perry C. Moberly and Margaret Ross. Perry Moberly was from the family for which Moberly Branch was named. Willie and Bessie Elswick's children are Katherine, Eva, Willie Moore, John Price, Lonnie, and Irene.

I personally remember Willie Elswick. He was, as I remember, a quiet, kind gentleman. He resided on Poosey Ridge Road, at what was known as the Perry Moberly Place, the home of his father-in-law.

Lewis Ward was prominent in my early years. He gave me my first hair cut, as I'm sure he gave many youngsters of that period. He also took me to my first movie in the early 1940's. Like Willie Moore, he lost his mother at an early age. I'm sure one of their disappointments was that they had no children. Lewis' father was Calvin Ward and his mother was Nannie Bell Locker. Their children were Ethel, Mary, Eliza, Nellie, Otis, and Lewis.

One of my joys is that I was able to see Willie Moore, Lewis and Lonnie again at the 1982 Gilead home coming after almost 40 years. It is also sad to say that during this writing, all three of these dear people have died. I trust that this writing will help preserve their memory.

Just north of the Les Long property on Poosey Ridge lived the Taylor Family. One of the greatest success stories to emerge from Poosey Ridge was that of the Taylor Family. The heroine of this story is Pearl Snyder Taylor, wife of Willie Taylor. Mr. And Mrs. Willie Taylor were the parents of fourteen children. The last, Darnell, was born in July of 1926.

The untimely death of Willie Taylor in early 1927 left Mrs. Taylor with the full responsibility of fourteen children. She accepted the challenge and succeeded in this Herculean task. On this small farm on Poosey Ridge, she fed, clothed and educated this large family.

According to her son, Frank, all who wished could go to high school and even college. Many did graduate from high school and some, in fact, did go on to college. I am sure that today many corporations could take a lesson in management from Mrs. Taylor. This was before the days of Welfare and Social programs, but even if they had been available, I'm certain she would have refused that type of aid.

It may not be fair to say that Mrs. Taylor ruled her brood with an iron hand, but it was firm to say the least. In addition to developing the character of her children through the values of hard work, honesty, and thrift, she did not neglect the spiritual needs of her family. She saw to it that her children attended church on a regular basis. I have heard members of my family tell about the routine of the Taylor Family getting ready for church.

The older children would help the younger ones get ready. As each one was scrubbed, combed, and clothed, they were commanded to sit on the front porch and not move until time to go. When everyone was ready, Mrs. Taylor would lead the way to the Gilead Baptist Church, approximately 1/8th of a mile up Poosey Ridge Road. When they arrived at church, she would see that the younger children sat in one pew while she sat in the center. You can be sure that order was maintained in that pew.

As in all families, especially when there are boys, there was occasional mischief. Mrs. Taylor was up to the task of dealing with it, however. Frank, one of the younger boys, shared some tales of his misadventures with me.

One of their barns was on the north side of the house so that a portion of the pasture or lot could not be seen from the house. Frank and one or more of the other boys managed to get a side saddle on a cow and attempted to ride her out of the view of Mrs. Taylor. The area where they were riding was close to the road and Mrs. Julie Moberly came walking by and began to reprimand them for riding the cow. They did not take Mrs. Moberly's reprimand too seriously and continued their adventure, that is, until Mrs. Taylor appeared. It seems as Mrs. Moberly walked by the Taylor residence, she took time out to stop and let their mother know what was going on behind the barn.

Needless to say, the boys received their just reward for their misdeeds.

Poosey Ridge is tobacco country, and most of the men either chewed, smoked or both. Naturally, boys also wanted to experiment with tobacco. Because it was socially unacceptable for young boys to smoke, they had to hide to do it. Frank related how he and his nephew, Manford Teater (Eva's son) and others managed to, as Frank put it, "get hold of some smoking tobacco".

They decided that the chicken house would be an ideal place to hide. One of the girls saw a light smoke drifting through the cracks of the chicken house, guessed what was going on and proceeded to tell her mother. The boys saw Mrs. Taylor coming and were astonished when she did not open the door but locked them inside instead. They watched through the cracks in the wall as she went around in back of the little house to some peach trees and began to break off some switches. She then had them come out, one at a time, to receive a dressing down. The others had to wait inside like lambs before the slaughter to take their turn at peach tree tea.

Even though the chicken house experience was very traumatic at the time, it only temporarily deterred the boys' quest for smoking. Frank, not to be deprived of the pleasure of a few smokes, hit upon a scheme to smuggle eggs out of the hen house to sell at Whittaker's store. During this period, eggs could be sold at the country stores for cash. Because of her large family, Mrs. Taylor most likely did not have any surplus eggs to sell. If she did, however, I am confident she had no plans to trade them for smoking tobacco.

Frank and his nephew, Manford, raided the hen house and put the eggs in Frank's hat, which he then put on his head so no one would be the wiser. As they started around the house, they paused to talk to other family members. Frank squatted down while Manford remained standing. I guess Manford could not resist the opportunity and slapped Frank on the head. The broken eggs ran down his face in streams of white and yellow. This was one time when Frank literally had egg on his face.

As was mentioned, there were fourteen children in this family. They are as follows (not necessarily in chronological order): Bertie, Eva, Josephine, Myrtle, Ova J., Willie B., Maude, Beulah, Homer, Gordon, Glenmore, Harold, Frank and Darnell.

In 1936, my grandmother, Annie Long, had her gall bladder removed. When she came home from the hospital, she was visited by her neighbor, Mrs. Taylor. When Mrs. Taylor returned home, she told some of her children about Mrs. Long having her gall bladder removed. Darnell, who was nine or ten at the time said "Well! She can't pee no more, can she?" This story was relayed to me by Beulah M. Howard, Darnell's sister, October 3, 1982.

One of my childhood playmates was Billie Jean Baker, Maude's daughter and the granddaughter of Mrs. Taylor. I can remember visiting Billie Jean when the weather was cool. We would get cold playing outside, go into the kitchen and sit behind the wood burning range with our backs against the wall. There always seemed to be a huge pot of pinto beans simmering on the stove.

The Taylors and my grandparents were neighbors for years. It was my pleasure to know Mrs. Taylor personally. The task this great woman completed, plus the impact she had on her community cannot be adequately portrayed by the feeble attempts of this author.

Mrs. Taylor passed from this life in 1963. It is my wish to share the memory of this courageous and iron willed woman with members of my family.

According to Frank, (Mrs. Taylor's son), Les became somewhat of a father figure to him when he was small. He said he and his brother, Darnell, used to follow Les around like pups. He enjoys telling humorous stories about Les and his day-to-day activities. He remembers when Les kept sheep on the property on Moberly Branch (I also remember this).

For some reason, Les had a buck sheep (ram) contained in a pen. Frank, Darnell and William D. (Les' son) were together quite often during this period. They would often be at the Moberly Branch Property. When Les was not around, they would tease the ram which in turn became rather hostile. Frank recalled an event when they were at the ram pen and Les climbed the fence into the pen to feed the ram. While he was bending over to put feed into the trough, as Frank put it, "the ram hit him a ton". When Les recovered from this surprise attack, he picked up the ram, threw it over the fence. Before the sheep could regain its feet, Les jumped over the fence and kicked it.

North of the Taylor property was where Willie Elswick lived. Beyond him, after passing the Dry Branch Road, was the Wolford Agee Place. Across the road from the Agee family lived Simp and Jessee Rogers. Jim Long said he remembered the day that Simp Rogers and Jessee Sowers were married. Jim said that he and others were stripping tobacco near the Sowers' residence when Simp drove up in a Model-T Ford to pick up his bride to be. Simp came into the stripping room and talked to them while Jessee was getting ready. Across the road from Whittaker's store, at 1216 Poosey Ridge Road, was a large structure known as the Les Curtis place. The first family I recall living there was the Horace Campbell family. The next dwelling south of the Curtis place was the Raymond Howard Property. My parents lived there for a short time after they were married, but my earliest memories are of Raymond and Jenny Howard living there. At the time of this writing, Stratton and Golda Howard Stocker, life long residents of the area, own this property. The house they live in is the house that Mrs. Stocker's parents, Raymond and Jenny Howard, lived in for many years.

In a conversation with Stratton in October of 1985, he shared some information with me about his father, Ellie Stocker.

Ellie Stocker and his family moved from Baldwin about 1913 and settled in the Poosey area. It seems Ellie was a man of varied talents. His veterinarian skills made him a much sought after man by the residents of Poosey to help heal and care for their livestock.

He also was an inventor. Ellie Stocker actually invented a one horse tobacco setter. It really did work. According to Stratton, Ellie never applied for a patent for this invention.

Ellie had a 1918 Buick, which was one of the first automobiles in Poosey. Stratton remembers the car was equipped with carbide head lamps. He said he can remember the family going to church in the evening when it was still light. Before going home, his father would light the lamps with a match. My father, who was born in 1912, has told me it was one of the first cars that he can remember seeing in this area. In later years, Ellie moved to Indiana. Stratton stayed in Poosey. Good for you, Stratton!

At the curve, where Poosey Ridge Road turns toward Round Hill, stood Cottonburg School House. Many of my relatives went to school there. Among them were Roberta Long and her cousins, Louise, Clyde, and Jewel Dean. Clifford Anglin also attended the school. Some of the teachers were Ophelia Estes, Mary Long, Marie Hubble, Ova J. Taylor, Betty Curtis, Nellie Isaacs, and Columbia Tussy. The next structure beyond the school was Click's store. This store was operated by Owen & Bertha Click. Their residence was next to the store building.

Chapter Fourteen

From the Hollow to Turner's Ridge

One of my mother's favorite stories occurred during this period, when she and Jim were living in the hollow. Les happened to be working in the area when a swarm of bees came very close to the house. He called for Ruby to bring him a dish pan and a large spoon. He began to beat the pan with the spoon and presently the bees began to settle on top of a fence post. As the bees settled in a huge ball, Les proceeded to spoon them into the dish pan. After this was done, he put them into a bee hive. Les had the ability to handle bees without fear of being stung.

Farm animals were always important to me, especially horses and mules. For many years, my Grandfather Les had a mule called "Old Dove". I remember this mule very well. It seems at this time, when someone named an animal, whether horse, mule, dog, or cow, they would insert the word "Old" before the given name. This word did not denote age, but rather affection. Some of the horses and dogs in our family were "Old Nancy", mare; "Old Frank", horse; "Old Bill", horse; "Old Snowball", dog; and "Old Bruno", Vernon's dog.

During the 1930's and early 40's, there were train loads of horses shipped into this area from the west. While in areas of level terrain, tractors were becoming popular, the farmers of areas such as Poosey still depended on horses and mules. These boxcar loads of horses were shipped into Richmond to horse dealers such as Lonnie Abrams who operated a horse auction.

Many of these horses carried brands which seemed unusual since no one in the area ever branded their livestock. Several of these western horses made their way to the farms of our families. There were three which I specifically remember. One was a black mare named "Nancy" that belonged to my father. She was a gentle, faithful worker. My Grandfather Long owned a small grey gelding called "Bill". For a short time, my father owned a bay gelding called

53

"Frank". Frank was mentioned earlier when the account was told of William D. and Charlie driving the team and wagon. There is more that can be and will be said about Frank.

Our family lived in the log house in the hollow until 1939 when we moved to the property of Bourbon Turner. This property was located in an area known aptly as Turner's Ridge, due to the fact that Bourbon and his sister Etta owned much property in this vicinity. Turner's Ridge Road turned to the left off of Poosey Ridge Road between the home of Willie Elswick and Dry Branch Road. There were several homes located on this Ridge Road. Proceeding out the ridge toward Paint Lick Creek, one can look to the right and see Dry Branch Road below, winding its way toward the same stream.

Some of the homes that were there in 1939 are still standing. Some are gone. What was then, the first house on the left is one of the survivors. When my family moved to Turner's Ridge, this house was occupied by the Irvin Davis Family. Irvin and his wife, the former Nora Warren were the parents of nine children. They are as follows: Jess, Les, Ed, J.W. (also known as Shay-bo), Cecil, Roberta, Laura Edith, Dorothy, and Fairy.

As a child, I became friends with Leslie Jr., and Carol, who were the children of Les and his wife, Jenny Belle King Davis. In the last few years, it has been my privilege to renew acquaintances with Laura Edith, Cecil, and Dorothy.

In the mid to late 1950's, Cecil Davis, his wife and mother, Nora, visited my parents at their home in Columbus, Indiana. I too happened to be present during this visit. Nora Davis told a story that I will attempt to paraphrase.

The Davis Family at that time was living on Poosey Ridge Road, just south of the Gilead Baptist Church. Many of the children had already married and left home. Her daughter, Dorothy and her husband, Paul Rhodus, were living on Dry Branch and were expecting their first child.

When Dorothy was in labor, the area was hit with a severe ice storm, making travel of any type virtually impossible. Nora, wanting to be with her daughter, made her way to the home of Les Long, who at that time lived across the road from the Gilead Cemetery.

She asked Annie Long if she thought she could make it to Dry Branch, and if so, would she go with her. Annie said she would be happy to accompany her, but they would have to take some precautionary measures in view of the thick layer of ice that seemed to have the world in its grip.

Before setting out on their precarious journey, the women prepared themselves by wrapping their feet in burlap bags, followed by wrapping strands of barbed wire around the burlap. The barbs on the wire served as spikes or cleats. They then drove a nail into the end of a tobacco stick to help them keep their balance and proceeded on in relative safety. The women arrived at their destination in time to see a healthy baby delivered and found the mother doing fine.

Poor Paul probably suffered more than anyone. Nora said she would never forget Annie's kindness to her and her willingness to be her companion through this harrowing experience. Annie Long died August 30, 1991 at the age of 95. Paul Rhodus was an honorary pallbearer at her funeral. He also told me the account of Annie and Nora as they braved the ice. Nora was active in the Methodist movement during its early days in Poosey, as was her son Jess and perhaps others.

I have visited Cecil Davis, who now makes his home in Madison, Indiana. We both enjoy reminiscing about earlier days in the Poosey area. Cecil is 8 or 9 years my senior and I can recall him in his teens riding his black mare from place to place. To repeat a phrase used earlier, "he was big enough to run around". Cecil became interested in a girl named Beatrice Long, who lived on Back Creek, over in Garrad County.

Cecil, who lived in the Poosey area, would ride across Paint Lick Creek and stay sometimes until the wee hours of the morning. When the farmers along Paint Lick Creek went to their barns in the morning, they were afraid to plunge their pitch forks into the hay or straw for fear of piercing Cecil who would seek out the soft, sweet smelling hay or straw to catch forty winks.

Cecil related a story about going to one of the many revivals at Beech Grove on Paint Lick Creek. As mentioned earlier, young fellows rarely went inside during these meetings. He, or one of the other fellows had a tube of red lipstick (who knows how or why). They began to battle (friendly) trying to see how much of the red substance one could get on the other. Of course each one tried to prevent the other from achieving this. Needless to say, in spite of his efforts, Cecil received his share on his face, hands, and clothes.

He later went to the home of his brother, Les who lived at that time on Poosey Ridge Pike. Before he arrived, it began to rain. When his sister-in-law, Jenny Belle, answered the door, she saw Cecil with streams of red running down his face and body. Cecil said, "She let out a whoop and said, "Lord Les, come here, Cecil's been killed."
The girl Beatrice, the object of Cecil's interest, did in fact become Mrs. Cecil Davis. After the Davis family moved away, there were several other families who lived there while we were residents of Turner's Ridge. Among them were Gordon and Etta Taylor and the Bill and Marie Murphy family. Mr. And Mrs. Denny Anglin, my grandparents, also lived in that house.

It was not unusual to see women of all ages travel via horseback as recently as the mid Nineteen Forties in the Poosey Ridge area. Very few women—especially older women—drove automobiles at that time. If a woman needed to go a distance of a few miles and had a horse available, she would think nothing of putting a common bed blanket or quilt on the horse's back, perching herself side saddle style, and going where she pleased. Hattie (Mrs. Elige) Prather was a frequent traveler by horseback during this period.

Hattie, who lived on Poosey Ridge Pike, just below and across the road from Miss Emma Sower's store, would ride from her home to her daughter Stella's home on Paint Lick Creek. The most direct route from where she lived was to go south on the Pike to Turner's Ridge, go past Mrs. Mollie Ross' place and down the hill to Paint Lick Creek.

On this particular day, Hattie was returning home via Turners Ridge when she met Jim Long and Bill Murphy. Both Jim and Bill lived on Turner's Ridge at this time. They were walking home from Creighton Whittaker's store where Bill had purchased a 25 lb. bag of flour.

As horse and rider drew near, Bill shifted the flour to his shoulder, causing the horse to shy and throwing Hattie onto a barbed wire fence. Hattie was not seriously hurt but received many scratches and bruises. She did not get upset at all but thought the whole thing to be funny.

The men helped her back on her horse and she went on her way. From that time on and for as long as she lived, every time she and Jim would meet, she would laugh and say, "Now Jim, don't you scare my horse."

When my grandparents lived there in 1942 and 1943, one of the events of that period was the making of sorghum molasses. My grandfather had raised sugar cane and decided to make the sorghum. This was somewhat of a community effort, referred to by the locals as a "stir-off". The term "stir-off" came from the process of constantly stirring the cane juice as it cooked over a fire. As the juice was cooked, foam would rise to the top.

People would fashion a flat piece of wood referred to as a sorghum paddle. When the paddle was dipped into the foam, it would harden into a candy like substance that was sweet and quite delicious. The entire neighborhood would be invited to participate and most of them accepted. It was a time of fun and celebration. Everyone had fun, except the poor horse or mule which would be required to walk in an endless circle turning the mill.

Chapter Fifteen

Getting Acquainted With Turner's Ridge

Proceeding out the ridge road in a westerly direction to the next road to the right, there was and still is a barn at the intersection on the left. A few yards beyond the barn there was a small frame house with several Lombardy poplar trees in the yard. Our family moved here in 1939. This property was owned by Bourbon Turner. He and his sister, Miss Etta Turner owned a substantial amount of land in this area, hence, Turner's Ridge.

I remember Mr. Turner well. He was a kind man as I recall, who would come to work from time to time to help maintain the property. He would bring his lunch in a large black lunch box complete with a thermos bottle filled with coffee. It wasn't unusual for Mr. Turner to generously share with me some of the treasures residing in that wonderful lunch box. In fact, he first introduced me to Ritz crackers, one of my favorites even to this day.

I visited this location in August of 1998. The original barn is still there but the house has been replaced by a modern ranch style home. There were many wooden farm gates on the various roads separating the properties. These gates remained closed most of the time because of livestock grazing in the fields. They had to be opened each time a motorized vehicle, team or pedestrian passed through. There was an ancient unwritten law which stated, if a gate is opened, it must also be closed. This law, even though unwritten, was rarely violated.

The next residence on the right, beyond where we lived was the home of the Dalton family, Charles or Charlie and Mammie Tussy Dalton. The Daltons were the parents of several children, many of whose names have been lost to my memory. Some of the names I recall are Lois, Bernard, Charles and Frances. I saw Frances a few years ago when she visited the grave of her brother Glenmore, at the

Gilead cemetery. I recall the sad event when this young man passed away while we were their neighbors.

I am reminded, as I write, the importance of opening and closing the farm gates discussed earlier. The Dalton property was owned by Mr. John Whitlock. When Mr. Whitlock would visit his property and I would happen to see him driving his automobile in our direction, I would race to open the gate for him to enter our property and then run headlong to open the gate to the Dalton property. Mr. Whitlock always acknowledged his appreciation for this service.

After passing the Dalton property, a sharp turn to the left led to the last residence on this road which was the home of Dave and Neva Foley Humes. Like the Daltons, the Humes boasted a rather large family. The Humes children that I seem to remember are Harold (I believe he was one of the older children), Melvin, Kenneth, Mary Earle and Anna Mildred.

Going back to the main Turner ridge road and continuing in a westerly direction to where a lane angles off the main road to the left leads to a home that was still standing and also a residence as of August 1998. During the period of which I write, 1939-1941 and early 42, the following families lived there: Homer Taylor, Willie C. Rhodus and Alfred Malear.

My father grew up with both Homer Taylor and Willie C. Rhodus. Their families have been or will be given more attention in this writing. Mr. Malears, as I recollect, lived there with his wife, their two sons Rayford and Harold and Alfred's mother who was known as Granny. It seems every household had an abundant supply of black berry jam and there were always biscuits left over from the meals. When my mother and I would visit the Malears, one of the first questions Granny would ask me was "honey, do you want a jam and biscuit?" Of course I would never refuse. The minute I would finish one, here she would come with another and another until my mother would become embarrassed. I also remember that this property had an ice house, one of very few in the community.

Upon leaving this property and going through another gate, the road angles to the right. The next residence on the right was the home of Bert and Pearl Rhodus Prather, along with their two sons Russell Dean and Cecil Francis. Bert, was the son of Elige and Betty Whittaker Prather. Bert's mother died when he was two years old and several years later Elige married Hattie Roberts. My memory is very clear of Bert's father and step-mother. Hattie was a kind and good natured lady. She was the same Hattie whose good nature was put to the test when her horse was scared by Jim Long and Bill Murphy.

Pearl's parents were James V. Rhodus and Lucy Sowers Rhodus. I also remember Pearl's parents very well. Lucy's father was Calvin Sowers. He owned property across Moberly branch from the Dan Long property written about earlier.

When our family moved to Turner's ridge in 1939, Cecil became my playmate. Cecil was the younger of the two Prather boys and nearer my age. It was always a treat for me to visit the Prathers because they had wonderful things such as a Victrola, with a crank to wind up. They also had records to listen to. In their upstairs they had an old phonograph which played cylinders.

Bert was a man of many talents, one of which was the ability to sketch. I can recall seeing drawings that he had made. He also played the violin (fiddle). I cannot remember how well he played because it was difficult to get him to play whenever we wished. Bert had a 1924 Model-T Ford roadster that I understand he bought new. This was a great car. I can remember on cold mornings he would jack up one back wheel before he would crank it to get it started.

Almost everyone who lived on the ridge had an automobile, usually 1930's vintage at that time. The ridge was a dirt road with no gravel. In the winter it was virtually impossible for a car with the wide balloon tires to negotiate that road. It was no problem for Bert and his Model-T, however. The two of them seemed to be able to go at will—even when the road was muddy. Bert kept his Ford in the barn, where I also recall seeing a buggy which was no longer used. He had a bay mare named Daisy who was getting along in years by this time, and from what I have heard was quite a fine buggy horse.

Besides the talents mentioned earlier, Bert also was quite creative. He made an item he referred to as a dumbbull. This was on the order of a wooden bucket or butter churn with a rawhide thong attached to the bottom on the inside. The thong was as long or longer as the cylinder was deep. After applying resin to the thong, one could grip it firmly in one hand, slide the hand slowly along the thong and produce a low, vibrating eerie sound that would send chills up the spine.

Bert has put his creation to good use many times on dark nights when young fellows in the neighborhood were hunting on the hillsides and hollows. He would step out to the top of a hill near his house or barn and begin to make the dumbbull talk. It is difficult to describe the low, unearthly sound that this relatively simple object produced, but it was enough to send many of the young hunters scurrying back home. Among them were Bert's neighbors, the Ross boys, Ira and A. J.

In all the years I spent on Turner's ridge, the memories of the hours I spent in the Prather home are happy ones, with one possible exception. It involved Bert's interest in being a bee keeper. There was a row of bee hives on one side of the back yard. During late spring and summer the boys and girls usually went bare foot. When playing in the Prathers' back yard it was quite common to receive a bee sting.

I would be remiss if I did not say that each time I visited the Prather home I was treated like royalty, especially by Mrs. Pearl Prather. When I was a child of five, six or seven years old, I am sure my behavior was not always acceptable, but one could never tell it from the kind treatment I received.

I recall one evening when my parents and I visited the Prathers. They had just sat down to supper (we had supper back then instead of dinner) when we arrived. We had already eaten and when Pearl asked me if was hungry, I said yes, over the objections of my mother. I have eaten in many fine restaurants over the years, but I do not remember any of the meals as I do this one very simple but memorable one. There was more to choose from, but I chose corn cakes fried in a skillet. They very thin and a golden brown. She separated the top from the bottom of the corn cake and added a generous amount of butter, which she had churned herself. She put the corn cake into a metal pie pan, cut the corn cake into squares and gave me a fork and a glass of milk. I had a feast, one I clearly remember until this day. The corn cake was large enough to cover the bottom of the pie pan. When I remember the kind people I have been privileged to know in my lifetime, Pearl Prather ranks among the top.

Bert died on December 18, 1968. Pearl passed away on March 14, 1953. I have said little about their other son, Russell Dean. Russell was much older than me. When I started to school in 1940 he was already in high school. One of the sad moments for our family was when Russell entered the service for W.W.II.

As was mentioned earlier, the property that my family moved to was owned by Bourbon Turner. The Prather property was owned by Bourbon's sister, Miss Etta Turner. Etta's niece (Ethel, Bourbon's daughter) would drive her out on occasions to visit the property. I remember Cecil commenting on Miss Ethel's big fine car. As I recall it was a 1938 Ford 4 door sedan. I am sure that during this period it did seem like a big fine car to both of us. I'm sure that Cecil would get a chuckle out of that memory today.

The last house at the end of this road was the residence of Mrs. Mollie Ross, a widow and her children. The children were Nellie, Elizabeth, Anna Lee, Ira, A. J., Cecil, John T. and Mildred. Mrs. Ross was the widow of Thomas (Tommy) Ross who had died several years earlier. I am only assuming that his name was Thomas. I have never heard him called anything other than Tommy.

The property on which the Ross family resided was owned by Brutus Cotton. The family lived on and farmed this land for many years. I was in this home many times as a child and remember Mrs. Ross as a warm, caring lady. It always took a lot of courage for me to visit the Ross household alone since they had turkeys and one old gobbler in particular seemed to think the front yard was his private domain. Each time I would approach the house and he was in the front yard, he would ruffle his feathers and charge at me at full speed. As a child of five or six, he looked as big as a barn.

Our family has always felt a kinship with the Rosses. I believe Mollie was the granddaughter of Albert Marion Long, my great grandfather's brother. Ira (Mollie's son) married Viola Oliver, the daughter of my grandfather's sister, Jenny. It was a sad moment for me when we moved from Turner's ridge and my association with the Ross family came to an end. One of my great joys, however, is that I have been able to renew my relationship with Cecil Prather. Cecil and his wife, Jane, now make their home in Mount Sterling, Kentucky.
Some of the Ross children were married and had left home when we were their neighbors. Nellie, I believe, was one of the older children. She married Charles (Charlie) Isaac. She and Charlie were friends of our family and attended the Gilead Baptist church as we did. For some reason, Ira, A. J. and Mildred are clearer in my memory than the others. Mildred, whom I believe to be the youngest, was a few years older than me. She and I, along with other school age children, would walk together out the ridge to Poosey Ridge Pike to ride the big yellow school bus to Kirksville school.

As mentioned earlier, my family moved to Turner's Ridge in 1939. I recall visiting the property before moving and it was occupied by a family named Howard. One thing that I thought was special was a dinner bell. It seemed to me, being only five years old, that it was located on a very high pole. There was a rope hanging low enough for me to reach it. I thought it very exciting to be able to ring the bell to summon my father home for the noon meal. The well was within a few feet of the enclosed back porch. It was an improvement from our previous home in the hollow which required us to carry the water quite a distance. Some of the memories that come flooding back are the people, events and even farm animals that shaped our lives at this time.

Chapter Sixteen

Snowball, Frank, Going to Mill and Christmas

Our dog was Snowball, or Old Snowball as we referred to him. Snowball was white, as one might guess from his name. He was a mixed breed shepherd type dog that was similar to a border collie in size and shape. I mentioned being reluctant to go to Mrs. Ross' home for fear of being chased by the turkey gobbler. When I had Snowball with me, however, I would stride boldly into her front yard. One word from me and Snowball would send the gobbler into the nearest tree.

I have already referred to my grandfather Les keeping sheep at the farm in the hollow. I do not recall the details, but at least on one occasion he decided to shear the sheep at our place on Turner's Ridge. The mechanical shearing blades were operated by someone turning a crank and someone operating the shears. After each sheep was sheared, it was immersed in an oblong box filled with sheep dip. This would kill the fleas, lice, ticks, etc. After the last sheep was sheared and dipped, someone had the bright idea to shear and dip Snowball. I did not like it very well, but we both survived. Snowball existed a while longer anyway.

Snowball would travel with us on Poosey Ridge Pike on the way to visit a neighbor or go to the store. He had a peculiar habit that eventually was his undoing. When an auto approached, he would leisurely trot across the road in front of the oncoming vehicle. He had gotten away with this behavior for several years, but one evening when we were walking home from Whittaker's store, his luck ran out. As we were walking past the Gilead cemetery, Roy Taylor, driving a mid thirties Auburn coupe came along. True to his habit, Snowball trotted across in front of him. It was getting pretty dark by this time and Mr. Taylor did not see him in time. Of course I was very upset by this turn of events and vocally blamed Mr. Taylor for this calamity. In truth, Mr. Taylor was not at fault at all. There was only one to blame, and that was Snowball.

65

During this period there were no tractors in use on the small farms in the hilly terrain of the Poosey, Silver and Paint Lick Creek areas. The power was provided by horse or mule teams. My father always seemed to prefer horses to mules for some reason. From the mid thirties to the very early forties it was common for train car loads of horses to be shipped into this area from the west. They were shipped to sales organizations such as Lonnie Abrams Horse and Mule Sales in Richmond. Many of these horses were branded, which was unusual to me since no one in this area ever branded their horses.

Of these western range horses, three made their way to our farm. The first two were a black mare that we called Nancy and a bay gelding called Frank. Nancy was a gentle, faithful worker, but Frank was another story. Frank was mentioned earlier when he was part of a team that William D. and Charlie were driving and Frank began to show his true colors. Frank could and would be a gentle and faithful worker for a while, but then for no reason he would become completely uncontrollable. When he decided to run away there was no fence in the country that he could not jump even if he was hitched to a plow.

My grandfather Les, had a grey gelding, also a transient from the west, named Bill. Bill was gentle and did not seem to be given to stubborn streaks. It was agreed that Frank should be traded for Bill. Since William D. was unmarried and was at the peak of his running around experience, Frank became D's personal mount. With Frank being ridden by D sometimes until the wee hours of the morning and also being worked all day long, he seemed to lose some of his excess energy. In a conversation I had with D shortly before he died, he said, "Frank could go in a short lope all day long".

My uncle, Luther Proctor, became the final owner in our family of this equine wonder. Luther did not seem to have any better luck with him than anyone else. In fact, he became so exasperated with him at one point that he shot him with a shotgun. The horse was not seriously injured because I doubt many shot actually penetrated that tough old hide. This was the last straw and Luther decided to sell Frank. He took Frank to the stock sales in Richmond and ran into a man who was interested in him. In fact he told Luther he would like to have Frank because he had one at home just like him. Luther said he thought to himself, "Lord help you".

Now we had a good dependable team, Bill and Nancy, that were with us for several years. Instead of having a farm wagon, we had a sled for transporting items which needed to be hauled such as tobacco, corn and other farm produce. One of the memories I cherish is of my father walking behind a turning plow pulled by the team and me walking behind him in my bare feet in the cool freshly turned earth. I can still almost recall the pungent smell of the newly turned soil and see the earthworms as they squirmed and squiggled their way back into the cool earth out of the way of the sun's harmful rays.

Like most of the small farms in the area, we also had cows, hogs and chickens. We had a red cow for quite a while I recall. In fact my Dad sold her and later bought her again. Our chickens were free range chickens, which meant they were not contained in a pen or what is commonly known as a chicken run. They ran free in the yard, fields and barn, but like Pa Dan's chickens, could always be expected to show up at feeding time. It was always a joy for me in the spring to see a mother hen who had hatched a brood that followed her along as she clucked to them. I was always fascinated when a storm cloud appeared because the hen would begin to cluck and spread her wings and the chicks would hurry to get under those protective wings. When she lowered herself gently to the ground, one could not see the little chicks even though there were 10 or 12 of them.

Through the years as I read or have heard read Matthew 23:37, I have been reminded of those events. Even though we had several hens which would hatch broods of their own, my parents would also order by mail 25 to 50 baby chicks. Baby chickens had many enemies on the farm. In addition to the cold, wet weather, there were weasels, rats, crows and hawks.

As it still is today, fried chicken was always one of my favorite foods. Today if one has a desire for fried chicken, there are a myriad of sources available. But to a farm boy, this delicacy was available only from the month of May to possibly September. Having to do without fried chicken from September to May, you can bet I made up for it throughout the summer.

For at least one year we grew corn in the field across the road from our house. I remember when it was cut, it was put into shocks called fodder shocks. We had a corn crib in the barn which held a good amount of corn. I recall one winter day that my Dad carried from the barn a #2 wash tub filled with ears of corn. He brought it into the kitchen which was kept very comfortable by the wood burning range. He, my mother and I then proceeded to shell the corn into the tub. The shelled corn was then transferred into a cloth 50-pound feed bag.

My father and I took the sack of shelled corn, mounted the grey gelding we called Bill and rode to Creighton Whittaker's to have the corn ground into meal. Just a few yards south, across the driveway from C. W. Whittaker's store was a mill operated by a gasoline engine. The mill was also owned by Mr. Whittaker. Les Prather was the miller at the time. This is where we took our corn to be ground into meal.

The fodder shocks remind me of a conversation I had with Santa when I was five or six years old. It was getting close to Christmas and the local newspaper, The Richmond Daily Register (now The Richmond Register) had well publicized when Santa was going to be in Richmond. Most of the farm families found it more convenient to go to town on Saturday and so it was with our family on the Saturday that Santa was going to be in town. It did not take me long to locate the white bearded, red clad, rotund gentleman standing in front of Lerman Bros. with a line of excited children waiting to unleash their list of expected gifts on him. When it was my turn to stand before his powerful presence, he asked the usual questions: my name, had I been a good boy, etc. Suspecting I was from a farm family, he asked if we had killed hogs. He said he was especially fond of pigs' feet and wondered if we had any. Because it was December, I told him we had already killed hogs and had given the pigs' feet to

Jeff Long. (Jeff was the brother of my grandfather.) Santa assured me he had been watching me and would continue to do so.

As Christmas Eve grew near, I wondered where Santa would be watching from. While I gazed out the window of our living room, across the road in front of our house, I was sure he was behind one of those fodder shocks watching every move I made.

Christmas during this time and in this location seemed far different than it does today. Today the Christmas season begins even before Thanksgiving and ends abruptly at the close of Christmas day. Back then, as I remember, the holidays did not begin until Christmas Eve and lasted through New Years day. This period was referred to as "Christmas week". My father was one of five children which were all married and had homes of their own by 1941 or 42. Each lady of the house felt it was her duty to have a Christmas dinner which was usually a noon meal. Of course, every one else in the family was invited. This included my grandparents on both sides, Les and Annie Long and Denny and Fannie Anglin.

From time to time, Les' brother Sam and his wife Omi, as she was called, would also host these gatherings. Sometimes it was difficult to fit all of the meals into one week. I have heard my father remark from time to time that he ate so much rich food during Christmas week a piece of cold cornbread tasted good. My grandmother, Annie Long, was famous for her boiled custard drink, which was always popular at these meals.

I can still recall some of the Christmas and birthday gifts I received while living there. One Christmas gift was a wind up metallic toy in the likeness of the Lone Ranger mounted on a rearing Silver. After being wound, Silver would prance around on his hind legs while the masked man twirled a lasso of wire over his head. A memorable birthday gift was presented to me by Miss Etta Turner. It was my sixth birthday on July 27th, 1940. My father happened to be at the Turner residence that morning and no doubt mentioned it was my birthday. She sent to me, via my father, what I have always referred to as a tiny Bible. It was only about two inches square and only a few pages containing the verse, John 3:16. I cannot be sure just how much I appreciated it at the time, but I have never forgotten it.

We only owned one automobile while residents of Turner's ridge: a 1929 Willys sedan.
This car was not around too long as I recall. We kept, for some time, a 1930 Chevrolet sedan that belonged to my grandfather Anglin. The Anglins lived at that time on the property of Mr. Holman Todd on Taylors Fork creek.

At that time, the Anglin family consisted of Denny, Fannie, daughter Ruth, son Clifford and from time to time Denny's mother, Elsie Garrett Anglin who the family referred to as Granny. The reason we kept Denny's car was none of the Anglins drove at that time. Saturday was the day that most country folk went to town, so we would pick up the Anglins each Saturday and take them home after a day's shopping.

When visiting the Anglin's, the most common route was from the Curtis Pike, up a very long hill past the Holman Todd residence on the left and down another rather steep hill which led to the back of the house. The house, a white frame bungalow style, actually faced Taylor's Fork creek. I recall around 1940 our family decided to visit the Anglin's before my grandfather purchased the car. The trip was made by horseback. My father rode the black mare, Nancy. My mother and I rode the gray gelding, Bill. She was in control of the reins while I, as a passenger, was perched behind her. As we descended Page hill and turned to the right toward Silver creek, we met the Homer Taylor family on their way home from Richmond. We stopped for a few minutes, exchanged greetings, and went our separate ways. We cut across the bottoms and joined Taylor's Fork just before it empties into Silver creek. Following the creek allowed us to arrive in front of the Anglin home and made the trip shorter by several miles.

I first began to know my great grandmother Anglin while she was staying with my grandparents. She enjoyed sitting in a porch swing and smoking a little stone pipe. I would sit with her in the swing and she would talk about the Civil War. I thought she was saying silver war since I was not familiar with the term "civil". We kept Granny at our house on Turner's ridge for a short time. It was during this time that our family established a long relationship with the Rev. and Mrs. W. R. Royce. We had them in our home several times while the Rev. Royce was pastor of Gilead. The Rev. Royce obtained a shoat (weaned pig) from my dad. Dad said he was never quite sure how this transaction went. He either gave Royce the pig and sold him the corn to feed it, or he sold him the pig and gave him the corn to feed it. He was never clear as to how it came out.

Ray Long
Taken about 1940

Chapter Seventeen

Back To The Hollow

We moved from Turner's Ridge back to the property on Moberly Branch, which was owned by my grandfather Long, in late 1941. I cannot honestly say I remember December 7, 1941 (Pearl Harbor), but I vividly remember December 8th. That Monday morning was unlike any I had ever seen at Kirksville School in the brief time I had been attending it. There were no classes as such that day. Everyone, grade one through grade 12, was assembled in the gymnasium. We were singing patriotic songs and listening to the principal explain what had happed and what we as students were expected to do to help support the war effort.

These were dark days indeed, not only for the Poosey area, but for America and the entire world. I became painfully aware of local young men who suddenly were no longer around because they had been called upon to serve their country. Some of the familiar faces that had been a part of my childhood and now were absent included Frank, Glenmore and Darnell Taylor, Kenneth Scrivner, Vernon Clay (Scrub) Ham, Russell Dean Prather and brothers Harold and Rayford Malear. Naturally there were many, many more, but these are just a few of the ones that come to mind. Thankfully, all these returned safely.

Banners with a star in the center began to appear in the windows of homes. These banners signified a member of that family was in the armed services. Americans began to do with less since many essentials were rationed such as food, clothing, shoes, gasoline and tires. There were no new automobiles made from 1941 to 1946. The very few 1942 models on the road were made before American industries concentrated their efforts on defense.

Radio was our ear on the world. Our news and entertainment came via our battery powered Del Rio radio that my father had purchased at Creighton Whittaker's store. We were always eager to hear the news concerning the war. The two most frequently listened to newscasters were H. V. Kaltenborn and Gabriel Heatter. We especially liked to listen to Heatter because he began his broadcast with, "there's good news tonight, or "there's bad news tonight". Our hopes were lifted when he began with "there's good news tonight", because more often than not there was good news. We could forget about the war for a little while by listening to such radio favorites as The Grand Old Opry, Renfro Valley, Lum and Abner and Gene Autry's Melody Ranch.

In our worship services at the Gilead Baptist Church, I grew accustomed to hearing comments like, "Lord, remember our boys today on the foreign fields of battle" when the pastor, deacons or laymen led us in prayer. Even the school children were asked to do their part for the cause of victory. An announcement was made at school that each student bringing in 25 pounds of scrap iron or metal to school would be treated to a ride in a jeep, driven by a real soldier. Jeeps had just recently been introduced to the military and the prospect of riding in one was very exciting. I had to steal every plow point my grandfather had, but I got my ride in the jeep.

As a result of the students' efforts, there was a mountain of scrap iron and metal on the front lawn of Kirksville School. The kids from that area really came through for their country. As I look back at this time in our history, I am filled with pride with how our country seemed to be 100% united behind the war effort. If anyone had even suggested protesting our efforts or burning a flag, I shudder to think of what fate might have befallen them.

Darnell Taylor had a collie type dog named Rastus, which was getting along in years when Darnell was called into service. The dog was visibly grieved when his master left home and did not return. Everyone in the community hoped Rastus would live until Darnell returned. I was told Rastus did live until Darnell returned home.

In our second move to the old log house in the hollow, I became more aware of the house itself. It had a massive stone chimney on its east end for the fireplace. Moberly Branch's source

73

was a spring at the foot of a hill on the Taylor property. The branch flowed southward until it made a 45 degree turn to the east not far from our house and near the well where we drew our water. I can still remember as a boy of seven or eight, barefoot and dressed in bib overalls. I would roll them up almost to my knees and wade up the branch, warmed by the summer sun, toward the spring. The closer I got to the spring, the colder the water became. By the time I arrived at the mouth of the spring, the water had become so cold my feet and legs actually ached.

I began to explore the area more on my own by climbing upon and walking on top of the many rock fences that crisscrossed the area. It was during this period that our neighbor, Lewis Ward, took me to see my first western (Gene Autry) movie. It was also during this time that I was called upon, albeit I am sure with some reluctance, to perform some chores. The garden was between the house and the branch, which flowed in the direction of Silver Creek. Once when I was asked to hoe the green beans, I hoed them on one side only. I remember my dad laughingly saying when I was old enough I would probably just shave on one side.

We raised tobacco on the back side of the property. At that time, it seemed quite a distance away to me. When my dad was plowing, hoeing, worming, suckering or topping the plants on hot summer days, it was my job to carry him water to drink. My mother would fill a small cream can or pail, which had a lid and a bail, with cool freshly drawn water from the well. I would don my cowboy styled straw hat, which was newly purchased at Whittaker's store, and carry the water to my dad, who by mid-afternoon (biblically speaking) received it joyfully.

Jim Long on Moberly Branch looking toward Hendren's Ridge

Chapter Eighteen

Whittaker's Store

I am reminded of an incident that involved my mother's straw hat. In those days when women worked outside, they usually wore a hat or a sun bonnet to protect them from the sun. There were fewer sun worshipers in those days than there are today. My mother and I were picking blackberries across the branch on the other side of the fence near our well. She was wearing an old straw hat that was definitely showing signs of wear. I saw my Dad walking down the hill in our direction. As he approached my mother, I was surprised to see him pull the old hat from her head and sail it into the center of the briar patch. Ignoring the scratches of the briars because I was upset with his unusual behavior, I plunged into the thicket to retrieve her hat. I returned, hat in hand to find them both laughing at my sudden reaction. I was astonished to see my mother wearing a new straw hat my Dad had just purchased at Whittaker's store. He had been holding it behind him when he approached us so neither of us could see it.

It was also during this time that I began to run errands for my mother. The errands included going to Whittaker's store to purchase small items such as a loaf of Honey Krust bread, a spool of thread or a box of baking soda. The adventure usually took place in this manner. In the early 1940's, eggs could still be sold for cash or traded for other goods at the country general stores. When my mother needed to make a small purchase, she would fill a Karo syrup pail with eggs. As I recall, this would be approximately 1/2 gallon. She then would write a note to the clerk listing the items needed. I was normally favored with a five cent candy bar as a reward for my services. With the bucket of eggs and the note, I would take a shortcut up the hill and come out on Poosey ridge pike just south of where the Ballard Scrivner family lived.

Even though it seemed far at the time, it was really not a great distance. It did not take me long to arrive at the store with its high porch in front. This store was built in the early 1900's when ladies rode side saddle and such a porch was necessary for them to be able to mount and dismount with relative ease. I walked past the porch and the single gas pump to climb the steps at the south end of the porch. As I walked into this well stocked country store, my eyes beheld its treasures. Among them was the soft drink cooler with bottles of Coca-Cola, Orange Crush, Grapette, Pepsi, RC and others submerged in 40 degree water. It seems to me that those drinks in that water were colder than the refrigerated ones of today.

This was indeed a general store because one could buy items ranging from yard goods, bib overalls, horse collars, horseshoe nails and plow points to groceries. There always seemed to be one or more loafers hanging around. The person behind the counter who seemed to wait on me most often was Neal Burnham Whittaker, Creighton's son. Neal would have been in his early twenties at this time. As I gave him the bucket of eggs and the list of articles my mother needed, he would read aloud the items needed and finish with "but don't give Ray any candy". Even though I had become familiar with Neal's sense of humor, these words still gave me cause for concern. With the few items that the eggs paid for along with a candy bar, I would retrace my steps back to our home in the hollow.

Since the R. E. A. did not come to the Poosey area until 1939, there were very few who had electricity in the early 40s'. Places like Click's store, Whittaker's store and the Gilead Baptist Church had electricity. However, most residences, especially along the branch and ridge roads that exited off Poosey Ridge road, did not or could not avail themselves of this service. Therefore, it followed that most people in the area still used kerosene or coal oil lamps.

There were a few people who had what was called an Aladdin lamp. This, as I recall, required a special fuel, had a honeycombed style wick and burned much brighter than the standard kerosene lamp. I remember as a child walking past someone's house at night and seeing a much brighter glow emitting from their window. The comment would be made, "these people must have an Aladdin lamp". Still, kerosene was a very important commodity to country folk. It was needed to fill the lamps as well as to help start fires in the stoves and fire places.

As was mentioned earlier, people could supply most of their needs from Whittaker's store, which also carried kerosene. Everyone had a coal oil can. The average size would hold about a gallon. There was a large cap on the top for filling the can and a spout with a screw cap to prevent the fuel from spilling out when the can was full. It seemed inevitable that almost everyone would lose the screw cap from the spout at one time or another. This was no problem for the resourceful Whittaker's, however. When they filled a can missing a screw cap, they merely reached into the potato bin or barrel and stuck a potato on the spout. It worked very well.

Country stores were a vital part of American life during the last half of the nineteenth and the first half of the twentieth century. I am sure they are still very important in certain areas even today. During the time of which I write, the country stores were a part of our lives. The stores and the local churches were the hub of our activity. There were three such stores in our area. Click's, was owned and run by O. E. Click and his wife, Bertha. This building was between the old Cottonburg school and the Click residence. This building is still standing as of this writing, but is no longer used as a store. Whittaker's store, was located down the road a short distance from Clicks. There also was Miss Emma Sowers store, which was further on down the ridge road.

The store my family most often patronized was the one owned by C. W. or Creighton Whittaker. The Whittaker family ran this store for many years. Everyone knew the Whittaker family on a first name basis. Creighton and his wife, the former Mable Teater, were the parents of six children who became familiar fixtures around the store. The children, as I recall, were Harry Dean, Neal Burnham, Franklin, Nelson, Mildred and Bobby. As I write this, I am reminded of something I have not thought of in years. Somehow, when bologna was introduced to rural America, there were those who gave it the name "dog". I can recall time after time an overall clad farmer walking up to the counter and saying, "give me about a pound of dog, Creighton".

These country stores were a necessity to the people who gratefully took advantage of them. Whittaker's store had one of the few telephones in the area. It was an oak crank type mounted on the wall. Many people would make their way from the ridges and hollows to place calls of various types. It was the benevolent merchant, such as Creighton, who was a factor in the survival of many farm families because he let them purchase their needs on credit. They would settle their accounts at the end of the year when their tobacco sold.

Whittaker's store was destroyed by a tornado in 1974, Neal B. was kind enough to provide me with a postcard size photograph of the store with a brief history on the back. The following is a paraphrase of the history taken from the back of the photo. "Built about 1904 by Robert Long for Les Cotton, a son-in-law. Merchants were Millard Campbell, 1918-1919, Cecil Broadus, 1919-1924, W. E. "Bill" Whittaker, 1924-1936, C. W. Whittaker, 1936-1947, C. W. and Nelson Whittaker, 1947-1954 and Neal B. and Nelson Whittaker, 1954-1974. The memories I have of this country store and the family that operated it during the time I lived in this area are special memories indeed. I want to thank Mr. Whittaker for the photograph and the memories.

Chapter Nineteen

Goodbye to the Hollow, Hello Dry Branch

Our second tenure in the hollow encompassed the greater part of 1942. One of my favorite places to play was the barn. The barn was located down a slight incline not far from the house and parallel with the branch. This was a very old barn, probably built about the same time as the house. It was a rather low structure but very long in length. It was a stock barn for all practical purposes with many stalls and mangers. The driveway seemed very wide which allowed lots of room to run. My grandfather, who owned the place, ran several head of horses, cattle, hogs and sometimes sheep on the place. There were fifty acres here and only fourteen where he lived on the ridge road.

As was mentioned earlier, my grandfather Long was a rather tall man and had limited patience with livestock. An incident I recall that makes me chuckle even today when I think about it happened in the driveway of the barn with my grandfather Les and some calves he was attempting to contain. Les, my father, William D. and I were all present. I was standing to the side, out of the way as the calves were being driven from one area to another. Suddenly a calf broke away from the rest and began to run up the driveway in the direction of Les. As the calf attempted to run past, he kicked at the calf hoping to turn it. Just as he kicked, the calf lowered its head, causing Les to miss. This action caused Les' leg to drape across the calf's back and the calf continued to run with Les hopping on one leg trying to keep up with it. The above mentioned incident is a classic example of Les' adventures with his livestock.

How many times have we said, if we only knew then what we know now? I remember in one dusty, cobwebby corner of the barn there was a strange looking saddle, just lying there collecting mold, and rotting away. I asked my dad what kind of saddle it was, and he said it was just an old army saddle. As I look back and remember the divided tree, I realize it was a McClellan saddle. That type of saddle was used by the Union army during the Civil war and continued to be used until the cavalry was mechanized. This part of the county was pro-Union, and I can see some saddle weary soldier riding into the barn, removing the saddle, throwing it into a corner and saying with disdain, "I hope I never see you again". The McClellan was constructed for the comfort of the horse, not the rider. If that saddle, even at that time had been cleaned, oiled and preserved, I wonder what it would be worth today.

It has been said there are certain smells and sounds that make an impression on children. There is one sound I became accustomed to in the old barn that I will never forget. That is the sound of a horse eating ear corn out of a wooden feed box. This is a sound, like Bert Prather's dumb bull, that is hard to describe.

There were two Christmas experiences that made such an impression on me while we lived in the hollow that I have never forgotten them. The first was when I actually had a visit from Santa one Christmas Eve. It was already dark outside and the stockings were hung by the chimney with care. A piece of fruit cake and a glass of milk were on the kitchen table as a snack for the red clad old gentleman when he arrived. Suddenly there was a knock at the front door. My dad opened the door and with feigned surprise saw Santa, white beard, red clad and complete with pack on his back. As in the Clement Moore poem, he said not a word but went straight to his work. There was a rather strong fire burning in the fire place and I reasoned that was probably why he chose the front door rather than the chimney. He opened his pack and removed my gifts. They consisted of the usual candy, fruit and nuts, a wind up toy and a farm set complete with red barn, white fences and farm animals. The wind up toy was a horse hitched to a milk wagon.

While all this was going on, I was standing to one side in wide eyed amazement. The Christmas tree that year, as in so many others, was a small cedar setting on an end table. The gifts were placed around the table. When he was finished, he headed for the kitchen to avail himself of the cake and milk. He seemed to know his way around. With a wave of his hand and a Merry Christmas, he left by the way he came in. It was several years before I learned my Uncle William D. had portrayed Santa so well that night.

By 1941, I had been bitten by the cowboy bug pretty bad. For Christmas that year I received a cowboy suit complete with shirt, vest, chaps, neckerchief and hat. I also received a black enamel six shooter that made a rather loud clicking sound when the trigger was pulled. Attired in my new cowboy suit and armed with my black enameled six gun, I would mount the Grey gelding, Bill, when he was available. Riding him bare back with only a work bridle, I would ride off in search of adventure. I would not ride too far off, however, because I was never out of the sight of my father or mother.

Another favorite pastime of mine was to coast in my red wagon. I would start near the back steps of the house and coast down the incline into the driveway of the barn. It was quite a thrill since the small hill would allow the wagon to gain enough speed to send me a good distance into the barn.

As was mentioned earlier, our chickens were free range. That is, they were allowed to wander wherever they chose. At feeding time in the late afternoon, whether my mother or father was dispensing the corn or laying mash, the chickens would come running in response to their "here chick chick". There was a very high hill in front of the house and there would always be a few hens at the top of the hill in search of whatever it is chickens eat. At the call for feed, they would begin to run from the top of the hill. The fat old hens would spread their wings and become airborne. It was comical to see them, unaccustomed to flight as they were, trying to stabilize themselves. If their feeble attempts at flying were amusing, their landings were laughable. They would try to land on their feet, but the weight of their bodies would sometimes send them end over end or result in a belly landing. It was always great fun for me at chicken feeding time.

In the fall of 1942, my father purchased a small farm on Dry Branch on contract from Roy Taylor and we moved away from the hollow. My father was 12 years old when his father bought the 50 acre farm from the Moberly heirs in 1924. My father had spent his teenage years here and had moved back on two occasions after he and my mother were married. Other family members had also lived here from time to time. I have often heard my Aunt Mary Laura Proctor comment when she thinks of home when she was growing up, this is the place she thinks of.

It was not a great distance from the hollow to our new home on Dry Branch. It was up the branch to meet'n house hill and then up the hill to Poosey Ridge Pike coming out in front of the Les Long residence. Taking a right turn, we proceeded down the road past Bellamy's lane on the left. There were two houses on this lane. One was the home of Duke Bellamy and his wife, Louvina, and Duke's parents, John and Belle Bellamy. John and Belle were the parents of nine children: daughters Mary, Flossie, Margaret, and Clara and sons, Hobert, Robert, John T., Duke and Branon. Duke and Louvina had two children: a son we called little Duke or Dukey, and a daughter named Lana.

The next residence on the left was that of the Taylor's. On the right was a rather new house that we referred to as Mrs. Taylor's new house. Mrs. Taylor did not live there but used it as a rental. I remember her son, Gordon, living there for a while as well as Les and Jenny Belle Davis and their two sons, Les Jr. and Carol. The next home on the left was that of Mr. Will Elswick and his family. The next road to the left is Turner's ridge and the next, Dry Branch road, which turns to the left down a rather steep incline. The stream begins here and winds its way in a westerly direction until it empties into Paint Lick Creek.

I have no idea how Dry Branch road came by its name. There was always water in it when I lived in that area. I think most would agree that Dry branch road was more improved than many of the branch roads in the area. It was wider and there were a few small wooden bridges crossing some of the small tributaries that flowed across the road into the branch. I cannot say I remember clearly each house and who lived there from Poosey Ridge road to Paint Lick creek, but I can recall most of them. As memory bests serves, I will attempt to recount the homes, families and other events that took place during the time my family lived on Dry Branch.

After descending the rather steep hill as the branch road exits off Poosey Ridge road, the road becomes quite level all the way to Paint Lick creek. There are several curves, however, as the road follows the contour of the stream. After reaching the bottom of the hill where the road turns to the right, the first house on the right was the home of Burdette and Marie Agee. The Agee's were the parents of two children, Royce and Barbara. I believe that Royce's name was actually Herndon Royce. Burdette was the son of Wolford and Etta Agee who lived on Poosey Ridge in the first house on the left going north just beyond the entrance to Dry Branch road. Marie was the daughter of Dave Long, possibly a distant relative of mine.

Just beyond the Agee property was a small frame house that was a rental. Luther and Mary Laura Proctor lived there for a short time with their two children. I believe this property was owned by the Hendrens. Proceeding down to where the road makes a turn to the left, there was a very old house on the right. My grandparents, Les and Annie Long, lived here in 1918. My great grandmother, Mary Campbell, who was Annie's mother, died here the same year. She was paralyzed from the neck down because of severe arthritis and made her home with Les and Annie the last few years of her life. As mentioned, this was a very old house. During the time we lived on the branch, it was in a state of disrepair. I have no idea how long it had been since someone had lived there, but I can't recall anyone ever living there.

Just a short distance to where the road takes an almost 45 degree turn to the right, there was a white frame house across the branch on the left. This was the home of the Elby Tackett family. Mr. and Mrs. Tackett were, as best as I can remember, the parents of seven children. They were Leslie, Helen, Harold, Gene, Glenmore, who was called Glenny, Angie and Carl. I apologize if I have omitted anyone, but it has been almost 60 years at the time of this writing. Glenny was near my age so it followed that we spent many happy hours together up and down the branch and across the hills. Gene also was a playmate and could be counted on for a fun time. We had all been smitten with the cowboy bug so we rode our stick horses and chased the bad guys through the imaginary wild west of Dry Branch. A few years after my family had moved to Indiana, I received the very sad news that my friend Glenny had died. He was still a very young man.

A relatively short distance down the road from the Tacketts on the left was our place. This small frame house and barn with a few out buildings was located on a narrow strip of land between the road and the branch. This was a small farm, most of which consisted of a hill on the right side of the road going down to what was known then as the Kelly or Marg Turner branch. The land leveled out quite nicely as it neared the afore mentioned branch and that level area became our garden spot. Directly across the small tributary from our garden and on the same side of the road was the home of Ollie and Ethel Casey and their son Clay. Even though Clay was a few years my senior, we spent a lot of time together. We would wade the branch and seek out adventure in the manner that country boys do.

The Caseys had either a late twenties or very early thirties Chevrolet. They would usually go to Richmond on Saturday and I became accustomed to seeing them pass our house with Ollie and Clay in the front and Ethel in the back. There was a connection with Ethel and our family. She was the daughter of George and Becky Prather, who lived on Poosey Ridge next to the Gilead Baptist church. George and Becky's daughter, Minnie, married Tom Witt. Tom's daughter, Lula, married Clarence Anglin, my mother's brother.

The Caseys were the parents of three children: Myrtle, Edward and Albert Clay. Sadly, Edward died at the age of eleven. Mary Laura Proctor shared with me that she and Edward both were born in 1917. She also advised me just recently that Clay's full name was Albert Clay. I had always known him by no other name than Clay. Mary Laura said Clay's father, Ollie, told her Clay was named for Albert Bogie and Clay Blakeman. My memories of the Casey family are happy ones. I was never in their home that I was not treated like a special guest.

On down the branch road a short distance from the Caseys and also on the right was the home of the Robert Warmouth family. This is the same place my grandfather, Les Long, bought in 1920. In fact, this was the first farm he purchased. The Warmouth's son, James R. would join Clay and me from time to time in our search for adventure.

As I recall, across and down the branch from the Warmoths were two houses. The first, I believe, is where the Robert Masters family lived. Both Paul and Edward Rhodus lived in the other home at one time. I believe Paul Rhodus lived there when we lived on the branch. There could have been a house or two other than the ones mentioned. At that time when one came to the end of Dry Branch road at Paint Lick creek, the road took a sharp turn to the left and crossed the branch without a bridge. This was an area that was known as Bradshaw's Mill because Les Bradshaw operated a mill here at one time. Many years before it was known as Pott's Mill. Upon inspecting an 1876 Madison County map recently, Potts Mill is shown clearly.

In Forrest Calico's great book, A HISTORY OF FOUR CHURCHES, he writes about taking corn to Pott's Mill on horseback as a young boy to have it ground into meal. There was a country store there which faced the creek. It was, as I recall, a well stocked country store. The merchant was Mike Bogie. Mike had a son named Curtis, who was called Curtie by those who knew him. Curtie and I were about the same age and attended school together at Kirksville and later on at Waco. I would say our family gave Mike a fair amount of trade while we lived on the branch.

There was a rather large white house between the store and the branch. It was the residence of the Clay Simpson family. Conditions changed in many ways as a result of our move from the hollow to Dry Branch. Instead of residing in a large two story log structure, we lived in a rather small frame house. The barn also was much smaller. There was no well, so we had to carry our water from a spring. We still had the same team of horses: the black mare, Nancy, and the gray gelding, Bill. I still had the pup, Snip, who had grown into a sizable dog by this time.

Sometime later, Snip disappeared and I never saw or heard from him again. There was an unwritten law which simply said if a dog is seen chasing or attacking sheep it is the owners duty to destroy the dog. It seems Snip was caught in the act and my dad asked my Grandfather Anglin to end his life of crime. It was probably 15 to 20 years later that my Dad told me what really happened to Snip.

Since Dry Branch road was improved, cars passed by from time to time. It was vastly different from Moberly Branch, which was not suitable for automobiles. The school board had contracted with Dave Humes to transport the Dry Branch kids to Kirksville school. Dave had a panel truck equipped with wood benches to sit on. Dave would stop in front of our house to pick me up. This was a great improvement since I was used to walking from Moberly Branch to the ridge road to catch the big yellow bus driven by Eph Croucher.

Chapter Twenty

Tragedy Strikes

In January of 1943, my grandparents, Denny and Fannie Anglin, and their son, Clifford, lived on Turner's Ridge in the house where the Irvin Davis family had lived. I always thought it was a treat to spend the night with them, but I was never allowed to do so too often. However, on the evening of Friday, January 29th, much to my surprise, my father asked me if I would like to stay all night with Pa and Ma Anglin. That is what I called them—Ma and Pa. Naturally I was delighted by these unexpected turn of events.

My dad and I walked up the road, cut through the Tackett property and up a rather steep hill to where my grandparents lived on Turner's Ridge. Even though it was January, it did not seem to be too cold. It was already dark. The moon seemed to be playing hide and seek behind some scattered fleece lined clouds.

The following morning when my dad came to get me, he made a game of trying to get me to guess what was new and exciting at our house. My thoughts ran to such as did the cow have a new calf? I did not think our mare Nancy had foaled. Did someone give me a new pup? I could not imagine. When I was told that I had a baby brother, I was stunned to say the least. During the last 8-1/2 years, I had been the only child.

When we arrived home, I found my mother in bed with the tiny baby boy. Turley Moore Long was born sometime on the morning of January 30th. The attending physician was Russell Pope, the same doctor who had delivered me in July of 1934. From the time that I returned home and for the next few days there seemed to be a cavalcade of people going in and out of the house. Neighbor women were cooking and taking care of the baby and others were doing whatever needed to be done.

The next day, my neighbor, Gene Tackett, came to visit. Gene remarked that Turley was pretty—for a baby. My mother got a chuckle out of that comment. Gene and I soon left the crowded house and went off exploring hills, valleys, ravines and streams.

I have often been asked, why the name Turley Moore? Turley was a well established family name in Madison County. The name Moore came from my mother's dear friend, Willie Moore Elswick Ward. I recall some of the women remarking there seemed to be a problem as the baby would not or could not take milk from the bottle.

The next day, Monday, February 1st was a school day and I went as was my custom. That afternoon when Dave Humse's small bus stopped in front of our house to let me off, I noticed an abnormal amount of people in and around the house. My dad was the first to greet me and gave me the sad news that little Turley had died. I went directly to my mother's bedside. She held me so tightly it seemed as if she was afraid to let me go. To say the least, that was a sad, sad day in the life of our small family.

The baby was taken to Oldham, Roberts and Powell Funeral Home and placed in a small white coffin. There were no calling hours at the funeral home and the body was turned over to the family for burial. The day of the burial was probably February 2nd. In those days, women who had given birth, were required to remain in bed for several days. As a result, my mother was not able to attend the graveside services. Before the baby was taken to the cemetery, my father carried the small white casket into the house and lowered it in front of my mother. She sat up in bed to view her baby for the last time. I did not attend the services but stayed home with my mother.

Gilead did not have a full-time pastor at this time. My records show a Willard Watts as pastor from 1943 to 1944. I'm not sure when Rev. Watts began in 1943, but at this time there was no full-time pastor. My father asked Neal Burnham Whittaker to handle the ceremonial duties of which he agreed to do. There has always been a special place in our family's heart for the kindness Neal Burnham showed us on that day. Turley was laid to rest in the Gilead Cemetery beside his great grandparents, Daniel and Laura Belle Long. His tombstone says, "Turley Moore, son of Jim and Ruby Long, Jan. 30th 1943 - Feb, 1st 1943".

As I was writing about this sad period in our lives, I was reminded how our many friends and neighbors came to our aid. The good people from Dry Branch, Poosey Ridge and Turner's Ridge could not do enough for us it seemed.

February of 1943 seemed to be a dismal period in the life of our small family. Shortly after Turley was buried on February 1st, I was hospitalized for about a week. I was having trouble with my stomach, which Dr. Russell Pope diagnosed as a liver problem and suggested I enter the hospital. I was admitted to Pope Hospital, the red brick two story structure on Second Street. I was in the hospital for several days. Although the term was not used, I often wondered if I might have had a mild case of hepatitis. I returned home and began to feel much better as the days and weeks progressed.

The Doctor suggested I might benefit from drinking goat's milk. My father purchased a goat and I drank goat's milk for a while. For some reason, my mother did not insist that I return to school right away. In fact, I did not return to school at all that spring. As I recall, it was a wonderful spring, filled with sunshine and warmth.

In the midst of those streams, hills and hollows there was always something for a boy to do. One of my favorite things to do at that time and for several years later, was to find a wild grapevine that had attached itself to the top of a tall tree. After it was cut at the base of the tree, the vine could be used as a swing. When using one of these swings, one could swing quite a distance if the conditions were right.

Chapter Twenty One

Happier Days

I had located such a swing across the road and up the hill from our house. The tree was located next to a small ravine, which might have measured five or six feet in depth. It was a dry wash and not spring fed, which meant there was only water in during rainy weather. I was proud of my swing and thought it was a thrill to swing across what seemed to be at that time a rather wide expanse.

One afternoon, my cousin, Vernon J. Proctor, and I were taking turns swinging across the rocky gully when we saw coming up the hill toward us, my Uncle Clifford Anglin. I cannot remember the details exactly as to how Clifford was dressed, but as we referred to it then, he was dressed up. He had on, I believe, a gray felt hat, dress shirt, tie and dress shoes. I can't recall if he had on a suit, sport coat or sweater. Under his arm he was carrying a box of checkers and checkerboard. He was on his way to Miss Emma Sowers' store to participate in a checker tournament. Clifford had the reputation of being a top notch checker player in that area.

He stopped to chat a while and watched us as we swung to and fro. He said he would like to try it himself, so he joined us in our fun. Clifford was always adventuresome and he made the suggestion that all three of us try to swing at once. As a rule, I was usually up for something different such as that, but for some reason this time I declined his kind offer. Undaunted, Clifford asked Vernon J. to swing with him on the same vine and Jay, as we called him, agreed to do so.

At this time, I think Jay was ten or eleven and a rather healthy youngster. I noticed as they began their departure, Jay's hands were placed above Clifford's on the vine. When they were halfway across the ravine, Jay's hands began to slip down the vine, forcing Clifford's off. At the center of the ravine's lowest point, there was a large flat rock. Suddenly, both riders released their grasp and plummeted downward towards the rock. They landed in a heap on the rock with

Jay on top of Clifford. Both of them laid there for a while, emitting moans and groans.

When they got to their feet and climbed out to survey their injuries, it was clear neither would require medical attention. Jay seemed to suffer less since he landed on Clifford. His appearance somewhat more disheveled than when he first arrived, Clifford gathered his checkers and board and limped on toward Miss Emma Sowers' store. Clifford, who is seventy six years old at the time of this writing, recently discussed this event with me. He remembers it clearly, as does Jay.

As winter began to loosen its grip and the warmth of spring began to invade the hills and hollows, the pain of what had happened in our family during the winter months began to subside—at least in my memory. Even though spring had begun early, I clearly remember April 1st, 1943 was a rather cool rainy day. As I was standing at the front room window wishing I could go out and play, I suddenly realized it was April fools day. What mischief could I contrive in my evil little mind?

My mother was busy in the kitchen as I called to her, "Mama!, the cow's out". I heard her mumble something like, "oh, that old heifer", even though she was not a heifer but an aged cow. I heard her put on her coat and overshoes and go out the back door. When she reached the front yard looking in all directions, I yelled from the window, "April fool!". Needless to say, she was not amused.

Because we had no automobile at this time, we did not get to Richmond too often. When we did go, we would go with my grandfather Les in his big flat bed stock truck or we would go with Roy Taylor from time to time. Sometimes I would be treated to a movie at the Madison Theater or a ten cent comic book, which most kids referred to as funny books because the pages were like the Sunday funnies in the Lexington Herald - Leader. These sporadic trips to Richmond were almost always on Saturday.

The Saturdays we did not go to town, I was usually given a dime. After a walk down to Mike Bogie's store on Paint Lick Creek, it was spent on a Royal Crown cola and a Payday candy bar. They were five cents each. I always looked forward to the trips to Bogie's store because there was always something to see or do there. Next to the store and near the road that paralleled the creek, was a rather long hitching rail. Frequently, there would be several horses hitched to it at once. That was exciting because it reminded me of some western movies I had seen.

Paint Lick Creek was the dividing line between Garrard and Madison counties. Customers would ride their horses across the creek from Garrard County to the store as well as from the hills and hollows of Madison. Gene Sabastian, whose family lived in that area, had a little gray pony with a western saddle. Gene, who was two or three years older than me, would let me ride his pony whenever we chanced to meet there. This alone was worth the long walk to the store. I also looked forward to seeing the Bogies' son, Curtis. Many a Saturday afternoon was whiled away down at Bradshaw's Mill at the Bogie store.

As a child, I was always attracted to horses. I had a small talent for sketching and horses were always one of my favorite things to draw. My father had always preferred horses to mules as a team and I have always been grateful for that. The team that was with us for the greater period of time was the black mare, Nancy, and the gray gelding, Bill. They were a faithful and dependable team. We also used them as riding horses even though they were not considered to be saddle stock.

Nancy was a small, but weighty mare consistent with the draft breeds and had rather large feet. My dad said the blood of Percherons flowed in her veins. In spite of her large feet, I learned early on that Nancy could run. I put her to the test late one afternoon, much to my chagrin. When the team had finished a hard day's work in the harness, it was customary to lead them to the branch for water. After they would drink their fill, they would be led across the road and turned out to pasture for the night.

93

On this particular evening, I asked my dad if I could ride Nancy up to the top of the hill where the grass was good and turn her loose. He said that would be alright on the condition I did not run her. He very emphatically said, "do not run her". Of course, I promised faithfully I would not, knowing all along that was the very thing I was going to do once I got to the top of the hill.

Nancy still had her work bridle on and Dad boosted me up on her bare back. He opened the gate and I proceeded up the rocky wagon or sled road in a slow deliberate plod. I am sure Dad was pleased with Nancy's slow, leisurely gait. When I was certain I was out of his sight, I broke off a low-hanging tree branch. I thought the switch would make a good riding crop. Nancy must have sensed what lay in store, because when she heard the leaves rustle she increased her gait.

The top of the hill was level and free of trees, brush, stones and the like. It was ideal, in my opinion, to fulfill the purpose I had in mind. I dug my bare heels into the mare's sides, spoke to her rather harshly and laid the switch to her rotund rump. She took off at a brisk gallop. I was amazed at how smooth she ran, because at a trot it was somewhat jarring. I ran her to the end of the level ground and back to the starting point. I slid off her back, removed the bridle and started back down the hill toward home.

Even though I had left Nancy in the pasture, I was still reliving the thrill of the ride. It was almost as if I could still smell the horse, feel the wind in my face and hear the sound of hoof beats. My joy was short-lived, however. Halfway down the hill I met my dad coming up. His words echoed in my mind, "do not run her". Down at the house he had heard the hoof beats. Looking up through the trees, he had seen Nancy and me as we dashed across the hilltop. I do not recall what we had for supper that night, but I'm sure I had to eat it standing up.

Chapter Twenty Two

Rex Peavine, Tobacco, a Faithful Mail Carrier and Goodbye to Dry Branch and Poosey Ridge

As stated earlier, horses were very important to me. They also were important to most of my family as well as to many, many others in that area. East central Kentucky was famous for its fine saddle horses. The Kentucky saddle horse became known for its beauty, comfort and stylish gait. When a registry was developed for this great horse, it became known as the American Saddle Bred.

In 1899 there was a colt foaled in Madison County in the Kingston area. Its registered name was Rex Peavine. This chestnut stallion became one of the most outstanding saddle bred horses in the history of the breed. He was a champion in the show ring as well as a sire. This great horse was owned by Dr. William L. Hockaday. The story is told that an eastern horseman signed a blank check and asked Dr. Hockaday to fill in the amount for the sale of Rex Peavine. Dr. Hockaday declined the offer.

In the early 1900's, my great grandfather, William J. Campbell, lived as a tenant farmer on the Hockaday farm. My grandmother, Annie Campbell Long, who was born in 1895, actually remembered seeing Rex Peavine put through his paces. In fact, I have a letter written by Annie in the mid 1980's telling me of one of these events. Rex Peavine died in 1925 and his off-spring filled Madison County with fine saddle horses. In fact the term Peavine among horses became so common that as a child I thought Peavine was a breed of horse. For example, my grandfather, Les Long, had a sorrel mare. When I asked him what kind she was, he answered, "she's a Peavine". Even years after his death, if Rex Peavine's name appeared at all in the pedigree, the owner was proud to call his horse a Peavine.

To some, the foregoing narrative might seem to be a departure from the events that took place on Dry Branch. When combined with the previous episode about the running of Nancy, however, I thought it might be the time to explain, if possible, the love affair that many in Madison County had with the horse.

That spring, as I recall, was mild. It was filled with sunny days and balmy breezes. These were busy days preparing the ground for corn and tobacco crops on the rocky hillside across the road. Just how much I personally added to this labor, I think, is best to remain unsaid. I went barefoot most of the time while my dad was working in the plowed fields. Needless to say, our feet would get very dirty during the day. Each night before bed, my mother would have us go to the branch, which was not far from the kitchen door, and wash our feet. My dad had tender feet and it was great fun for me to see him gingerly make his way to and from the branch on the rocks.

One thing that has all but disappeared from country homes is the water bucket and dipper. Every home had a water bucket family members as well as guests drank from with a common dipper. No one thought anything about it, that's just the way it was. The lady of the house always tried to keep fresh water from the spring, well or cistern available at all times. It was good to be able to walk up to the water bucket and deeply drink the cool water from the dipper.

Another very important part of farm life was a vegetable garden. It was necessary to raise the much-needed produce for canning. A large potato patch also was important. After being dug, potatoes would last quite a while if stored properly in a cool dry place. Sometimes they were buried where the ground was dry, such as in a barn or shed.

Our garden spot was down the road on the right, near the Marg Turner, which was sometimes called Kelly Branch. It was just across this same branch from the Ollie Casey home. I was with my dad as he was preparing the ground for our garden. The ground had been plowed and an A harrow had been used to break up the clods. The ground was now ready for the drag to smooth the dirt so it could be laid off in rows for the planting.

The team, Bill and Nancy, had been used in all of these procedures and was now hitched to the drag. The drag, which was a home made device, was nothing more than a platform made of boards or small logs. The important thing was that it needed to be heavy enough to smooth the dirt. As I recall, one or more large flat limestone rocks had been added for extra weight. Dad was standing on the drag driving the team and I was sitting at the front where the team was hitched. The old western style straw hat I was wearing was beginning to show its age and I thought I deserved a new one. My parents did not agree, however, and said new straw hats cost money and besides, the one I had was plenty good enough. As I rode the drag, I took off my hat. While I was looking at its worn and tattered areas, a plan began to formulate in my mind. If I laid the hat on the very front edge of the drag, and it slipped off and was run over, I certainly could not be blamed. It would be an accident, and I would feel terrible, but would surely be rewarded with a new hat. So I put my hat on the front edge of the drag and began to work up the courage to push it off. I rode the drag in that position until my father had finished dragging the entire garden, but I never found the courage to destroy my old straw hat.

As with most farms in the area, we had a tobacco base. This was the cash crop the farmers depended on from year to year. We also raised corn. There wasn't enough corn to sell, but sufficient to feed the livestock. As I write this narrative, I find myself in the computer age. It is a very high-tech society. It is a world where technology seems almost out of control.

There are some who might disagree with this statement, but I believe I witnessed a technological change in the method of tobacco cutting in that area in the early 1940's. My very early memory recalls a tobacco knife with a cutting blade affixed to the end of a metal rod and a wooden T-handle for the worker to hold on to. The tobacco stalk was cut by a downward thrust, the pressure being applied to the T-handle. The same knife was used to split the stalk from the top almost to the bottom so the plant might be placed on the stick.

97

In the early forties, I began to notice a change in the method of cutting tobacco. Instead of the old style T-handle knife, farmers began to use a hatchet type cutting device they called a tomahawk. They no longer split the stalk with the knife, but used a metal cone shaped item with a very sharp point that was called a spear. It was placed over the end of the tobacco stick and the stalk was forced over the spear.

This change in technology considerably sped up the process. However, as in all technological changes, there was a painful transition period connected with this learning process. During this time, it was quite common to see a man with a bandage on the palm of his left hand and/or a bandage on the calf of his left leg. The location of the bandages depended on whether the worker was right or left handed. Unaccustomed to these new tools, men were continually piercing their hands with the spear, or missing the stalk with the tomahawk and cutting their legs. I suspect there have been even more technological advances in the housing of tobacco since the advent of the tomahawk and spear.

A very familiar figure I became accustomed to seeing on an almost daily basis was that of Mr. James V. Rhodus. Mr. Rhodus was our mail carrier when we lived on Dry Branch. Mr. Rhodus did not stop at each house along the way because there was a collection of mail boxes at the curve across from the Tackett residence. He would pick up the mail from Miss Emma Sowers' store, which also served as a post office, deliver it up the ridge road, down Dry Branch and eventually across Paint Lick Creek.

I have a letter from his grandson, Cecil F. Prather, dated January 2, 1982. It describes how during inclement weather or when the creek was up, Mr. Rhodus would deliver the mail via horseback. When he wasn't using his horse, he would drive his car, which I believe was either a 1934 or 35 Chevrolet sedan. Mr. Rhodus rode an easy gaited bay mare he referred to as his saddle mare.

My earliest memories recall Mr. Rhodus and his family. He was a long-time member and a deacon of the Gilead Baptist Church. His home was near Miss Emma Sowers' store on Poosey Ridge Pike.

I believe Mrs. Rhodus and Emma Sowers were sisters. Mr. and Mrs. Rhodus were the parents of nine children. They are, not in chronological order: Pearl, Bessie, Hugh, Eugene, Sherman, Edward, Cecil, Willie C. and Paul. We were neighbors to Willie C. when we lived on Turner's Ridge and to Paul when we lived on Dry Branch. This was just one of many families who touched our lives when we lived in this area.

Dry Branch was considered a small stream at best with the majority of its winding course being rather shallow. However, there were at that time areas people referred to as holes of water. To an adult, these holes were not very deep, but to a boy nine or ten years of age it was not unusual to find one at least waist deep.

July 27th, 1943 represented my ninth birthday and still is very clear in my memory. That was the day I learned to swim in Dry Branch. My father was never one to spend time fishing, but on this particular day he did agree to help some fellows seine the lower part of the branch near where it empties into Paint Lick Creek. There were probably three or four involved in this venture, but I do not recall who they were with the exception of Robert Simpson. I do remember Robert was part of the group.

While the fishermen were busy casting their net, I explored an area of the branch I had never visited before. I was wading in an area that was about knee deep when it suddenly dropped to a pool about waist deep for ten to fifteen feet before it resumed its knee high level again. Where we lived, back up toward the source of the branch, the stream was shallow and narrow, and there was no way even a boy could swim in it. But the closer it got to Paint Lick Creek, the deeper and wider it became. I thought it would be wonderful to learn to swim, so I began to run from the shallow water into the deep, falling forward with arms and legs flailing attempting to stay afloat. I tried this procedure several times and began to notice I was going farther each time before my feet touched the bottom. When I left that hole of water I felt very satisfied. I might have been dog paddling, but I swam. I doubt very much I could go back to that spot today. But if I could, I am sure I would wonder, "how did I ever learn to swim in that"?

I have talked to school children today and they tell me their summer vacations pass very quickly. Of course the seasons also come and go rather rapidly for me now, but I attribute that to the fact I am growing older. In those bygone years when I was a child, the summers seemed to go on and on. The summer of 1943 did come to a close, but the beginning of school was delayed for a few weeks. WWII was at its peak and many of the able bodied young men who made up the work force for farm labor was in service. The school board decided to delay the opening of the county schools in early September so the boys, and girls who were old enough were available to help get the tobacco cut and housed. As I recall, there was school on Saturday for a while to imake up for the time lost.

I did return to Kirksville School that fall, but did not complete the fall term. By this time my father had decided he had had enough of farming. He was thirty one years old, had been on the farm his entire life and thought it was time to try something else. We had an auction sale of our household goods, livestock and virtually everything. I was told that Eph Croucher bought the gray gelding, Bill. I am not sure who bought Nancy. We moved to Lancaster Pike, which was three miles from Richmond. After a short stint with the county highway department, my father went to work for the Kentucky State Highway Department.

Chapter Twenty Three

Poosey Physicians

The medical profession was—and I am sure still is—well represented in the Poosey/Silver Creek area. However, the medical services were more local in the 1940's than they are now. There were physicians who lived and practiced in the community. The following physicians are certainly not a complete list of those who attended the physical needs of the people in this area, but only a few of the ones I am aware of by reputation and personal contact.

In Forrest Calico's fine book, "A Story Of Four Churches", he refers to Dr. Oliver Perry Sallee, 1801-1877. Calico's comment was that it was said that the Doctor never made a call that his wife, Phoebe Tudor Sallee, did not try to put a clean shirt on him.

Even though I never met him or to my knowledge saw him, a name that is very familiar to me is that of Dr. W. K. Price. I have heard my family talk of Dr. Price all of my life. At one time, my father owned a small racking horse named Rex which once belonged to Dr. Price. Dr. Price delivered two of Les and Annie Long's five children, Vernon and Mary Laura.

Parents at that time often named their children after the doctors who delivered them. I am reminded of men in that area such as Price Agee, Robert Price Whittaker and others. Although I have nothing documented, I have no doubt these men were named after Dr. Price. This good doctor attended to the medical needs of this community for many years and also served as county judge for a period of time. Because Dr. Price touched the lives of so many and was such an influence in this community, this meager tribute is not adequate.

The physicians who were the most prominent in our family during this period were Dr. H. C. Pope and his sons Russell and Mason. The statistical information offered here on these men of medicine was gathered from the book, "Glimpses of Historic Madison County, Kentucky" by Jonathan T. and Maud W. Dorris. This great book states that "Dr. Henry Cook Pope graduated from the Louisville Medical School in 1906, located in Kirksville, and did general practice in Madison and Garrard counties".

Dr. Pope opened a drug store in Kirksville where he also maintained his office and received patients. As I recall, his residence was next door to the drug store. I have in my possession a photograph of Dr. H. C. Pope sitting in his back yard at Kirksville. The photo was taken by Roberta Long in 1940.

Dr. Pope had two sons: Russell Lee and Mason Glenmore. Like their father, they both chose the medical profession. Again, lifting information from the Dorris book, Russell graduated from Greenbrier Military School in 1926. He obtained pre-med training at Eastern Kentucky State College in 1928 and graduated from the Louisville School of Medicine in 1932. Mason, on the other hand, graduated from Kentucky Military Institute in 1928, from Eastern Kentucky State College in 1932 and from the University of Tennessee in 1935. He interned at Waterbury, Connecticut for one year.

According to Dr. and Mrs. Dorris, "The father and two sons purchased from Mr. Jim Culton and wife a lot on North second street, Richmond, Kentucky and erected in 1939 the Henry Cook Pope Hospital". The book goes on to describe how the hospital was equipped and mentioned by name some of the staff. The hospital began to receive patients January 3, 1940.

Most of the previous information about the Pope doctors was documented in the excellent Dorris volume. However, the following is based on what I have heard from family members or have experienced personally. The Long family has been the recipient of the Pope's medical services since the early part of the last century. My father, Jim, was delivered by H. C. Pope in April of 1912. His brother, William D., was delivered by Dr. Pope in June of 1923 and his sister, Roberta, was delivered by Dr. Pope in February, 1926. I was delivered by Russell in July of 1934 as was my brother in January of 1943.

My father has told me many times that he always felt like he and his brother, Vernon, practically grew up with Russell and Mason. When Dr. H.C. Pope made a house call on the Les Long family, he would often take his two sons with him. While the good doctor was ministering to the family's physical needs, Jim, Vernon, Russell and Mason would play along Moberly Branch or spend their time climbing in the barn. In this bygone era, doctors making house calls was the rule rather than the exception, so the Pope boys made several visits to the Long household.

Years later, my family chose Russell as our personal physician. I recall going with my mother to the Pope Hospital to visit Russell at his office. Whether my mother was sick, I was sick, or both of us were ill, I always seemed to accompany Mom on these trips. There was a waiting room just inside the front door that always seemed to be packed with people. When it finally was our turn to be ushered into his office, I was always amazed at the many figurines of horses on his desk, shelves and other areas. On most occasions he would give me one of the small figurines, which would delight me. I remember at the end of one visit he gave me two rather large firecrackers on the condition my father would light them for me.

Russell was not only a collector of horse figurines, he was a true horse lover and owned many fine blooded saddle horses. The following is a story that I have told my children and now my grand children that they cannot conceive of in this day and time. In early 1944 I needed a tonsillectomy. The appointment was made and my parents and I were to be at the hospital at 10:00 on a certain morning. When we arrived at the hospital Dr. Russell had not yet appeared. My mother went inside while my dad and I waited outside in the parking lot for Russell's arrival. We had not waited long before we saw him coming along Second Street astride a beautiful sorrel horse. He was dressed in jodhpurs, boots and complete riding regalia. He rode around to the rear of the hospital, tied his horse to a tree and the three of us walked into the hospital together. A few minutes later he removed my tonsils. My father said after he was finished with me, he got back on his horse and rode away.

The last time I saw Dr. Russell was in the spring of 1945. Our family had moved to Lancaster Pike, three miles west of Richmond.

Russell had rented pasture for some of his horses across the road from where we lived. He had driven down an unpaved lane rather late one evening to check on his livestock. It had recently rained and his car became stalled in the mud. Knowing where we lived, he walked to our house to phone for help.

Russell was very sincere and dedicated to his medical profession. However, when he was away from his craft, he had a tendency to be less serious. When he phoned for help and was asked where he was stalled, he replied, "I'm out here on the Green River Road". We all laughed when he replied in this fashion because there was no Green River Road or Green River in Madison County. I do not recall how he communicated to the person with whom he was talking where he was precisely, but he was soon rescued from his dilemma.

It was a very sad day in the life of our family when we received the news of Russell's death on October 14th, 1945. He died as the result of an automobile accident on Big Hill Avenue in Richmond. He was thirty seven years old.

Dr. Mason G. Pope was called to active service in W.W.II in January of 1943. I have in my possession a scrapbook my grandmother, Annie Long, began about 1940. There is a photograph along with an article clipped from the Richmond Daily Register showing Captain Mason Pope in his helmet with the medical cross on it. The article stated he was home on furlough and afterwards he was to report for duty at Camp Atterbury, Indiana. This article was dated August, 1944.

After Russell's death, Mason took over the surgery at Pope Hospital. There were other hospitals in Richmond, but it seems our family as well as a good part of the population of Poosey Ridge chose Pope Hospital to meet their medical needs. As noted in the portion of this writing devoted to Dr. Price, people often named their children to honor the family physician. In the Poosey area there were scores people named Russell, Lee or Glenmore. All of the previously-mentioned physicians had a special place in the hearts of the people in this area.

Chapter Twenty Four

Churches

Gilead

Gilead Baptist Church has been a part of the Poosey Ridge community for at least 200 years. In Gilead's two century existence it has experienced both feast and famine, yet it has endured. It is likely that the infusion of sturdy pioneer stock has given Gilead Baptist its substance. Among the pioneers was Lewis Craig.

Although Craig was not personally involved with Gilead, indirectly he had a great influence on this church. Craig was born around 1737 in Virginia. He was raised on a farm and began to preach sometime after 1765. He was associated with the Regular Baptists of Virginia as well as the Gilbert's Creek Baptist Church.

At this time Virginia had some very rigid laws concerning preaching and corporate worship. Feeling restricted in their witness, Craig and the entire Gilbert's Creek Church decided to move west into Kentucky. This congregation became known as the walking church and settled in what is now Garrard County in 1781. The Gilbert's Creek Church was the third organization of its kind in Kentucky and served as a launching pad for other new churches in the area. The old Kentucky pioneer, Daniel Boone, moved west of the Mississippi in 1795, and a small church had been constituted at the mouth of Silver Creek in Madison County to move to the Illinois Country. A few small churches were constituted that year.

Much of the above information was lifted from Spencer's History of Kentucky Baptists.
It seems reasonable that one of those could have been Gilead and another Salem Christian Church. There seems to be little doubt that Gilead has been in existence since around 1795. The records show Gilead joined the Tates Creek Association in 1806. According to the French Tipton papers, which are in the possession of Eastern Kentucky University, Gilead joined Tates Creek in 1806 with a total

of 18 members. In Forrest Calico's book, "A Story of Four Churches", he states that Edward Turner, a Baptist preacher, son of John Turner, organized the first church here and was a delegate to the Tates Creek Association in 1806. It is interesting to note, however, that a list of pastors in the Gilead record books show the first pastor as Edward Tudor in 1806.

In his book, Calico reports that Gilead Baptist Church is located on Poosey Ridge Road, (formerly known as Goggin's Ferry Road) approximately four miles north of Kirksville. Kirksville was known as Centerville until around 1855. Calico goes on to say the land on which the original church was located was owned by Green Clay. Clay sold the property to Jacob Baker and he sold it to Travis Million. In 1818 John Tudor became owner of the property. In the division of Tudor's estate in 1851, his son, Mark, and his wife, Fatima, are mentioned. In addition to Mark and Fatima, Gilead Church lot also is mentioned for the first time. It's possible there was never a deed to the original lot.

Those of us who have an interest in the history of Gilead will always be grateful to Forest Calico and his very valuable book, "A STORY OF FOUR CHURCHES". It is unclear exactly how many church buildings there have been. Local history says there was a log structure in the northwest corner of the present graveyard which was used jointly as a house of worship and school. Again borrowing from Calico, he states that a new church was built in 1842. In 1850 or a few years later, Calico says yet another building was constructed. This building endured until the present building was constructed in 1892.

Miss Betty Curtis shared that her mother, Mrs. Nannie Tussy Curtis, told her she remembered the old church when she was a child. She said it stood in the center of the present cemetery approximately where the flag pole now stands. Mrs. Nan Curtis lived to the mid 1980's, her age being well over 100 years. Residents of that area began to bury their dead early on in the old section of the cemetery, the northern half. There are some very old markers there in addition to many unmarked graves.

Probably by 1850 the north end of the present cemetery was beginning to fill up since there had been burying there for 50 years or more. I have in my possession a copy of a deed dated May 10, 1877. It shows that Allen Taylor and his wife, Josephine, deeded to the trustees of Gilead Baptist Church, one acre of land adjoining the original lot. The trustees were Nathaniel Cotton and Jacob Moberly.

It was not specified on the deed exactly how the property was to be used. The deed only said it was for the benefit of the church. It is reasonable to assume the Taylors might have thought a new building would be constructed on the property. However, it was another 15 years before a new building was constructed and it was not built on this property. People began to bury in the new area long before it was considered to be a part of the cemetery. Allen and Josephine Taylor were the parents of Willie Taylor, who with his wife, Pearl Snyder Taylor, were the parents of fourteen children. The Taylor family has been mentioned in more detail in another section of this writing.

There is a ledger at Gilead with a list of pastors from 1806 to 1978. There were 44 pastors in a period of 172 years. Possibly no other man had more influence, or length of service at Gilead than John G. Pond. The church records show Pond was pastor from 1871 to 1884, and I am sure this is true. However, the Tates Creek Association minutes, which are now in the library of the Southern Baptist Theological Seminary in Louisville, records a meeting being held at Gilead in 1852 listing John G. Pond as pastor. There are other Tates Creek records that show Pond as being pastor of Gilead, Centerville (Kirksville) and Drakes Creek at the same time. Again, quoting Spencer's History of Kentucky Baptists he states that "John G. Pond is one of the oldest and most prominent ministers of the Tates Creek Association, of which he has been moderator for some years past".

At the beginning of the Civil War, Pond recruited a company of the eleventh Kentucky cavalry from men mainly in this area which was pro-union. Madison County was divided almost in half, the northern half being Union and the southern half Confederate. This company became known as "Pond's Cavalry". After the war Rev. Pond became known as Colonel Pond to the local residents. It has been my privilege to have known two of Colonel Pond's great grand daughters: Ruth Ross Mahanes, a resident of Garrard County, and Lina Pond, who was born in Round Hill, but moved to Deputy, Indiana with her family in 1915. These two ladies have given me much interesting information about the old Colonel.

I have in my possession a copy of a document showing where Gilead was re-organized and constituted as a United Regular Baptist Church. This document is dated September 3, 1842. Up to this time the church had been affiliated with the Separate Baptists. The constitution was revised in 1894, signed by a committee of two: J. P. Long and H. M. Snyder. The growth from this time on was slow but steady. The following is an account of some of Gilead's accomplishments from 1852 to 1902 as recorded in the minutes of the Tates Creek Association's annual sessions.

August, 1852
Pastor: John G. Pond
Messengers: M. B. Willis, William Cotton, H. Elkin, J. Williams, and J. Calico,
(probably James Calico, Morris Calico's father).
Minutes showed:

Baptisms————0
Received by letter—0
Dismissed——0
Excluded————0
Died—————0
Total Members-40

August 25, 1874—11:00 A. M.
Pastor: John G. Pond
Messengers: T. B. Tudor, D. Tudor, J. Hendren, Nate Cotton and J. M. Cotton
No minutes recorded.

August 27, 1895
Pastor: A. J. Pike
Messengers: Nate Cotton, Snyder, Alex Tudor, Robert Long, Robert Tudor,
> Sidney Tudor and William Hendren

Baptisms—80
Total Members—253

August 26, 1902
Pastor: A. J. Pike
Messengers: J. P. Long, Nate Cotton, W. B. Coy, H. M. Snyder, R. Ross,
> David Long and Robert Long

Baptisms—18
Excluded—68
Received by letter—14
Deaths——2

The Civil War took its toll on this area as it did all of Kentucky as well as the eastern half of the United States. As was mentioned earlier, John G. Pond was instrumental in organizing a portion of company A of the 11th Kentucky Cavalry comprised largely of recruits from this area. Turner Barnes was pastor in 1862 and Moses Willis in 1865.

According to Forest Calico, the only two men at Gilead during this period were William "Buck" Cotton and James Calico. The church used the building, which was erected about 1850, until the present edifice was completed in 1892. The property for the site of the present building was purchased April 15, 1892, from Alex and Margaret Ray. This same Alex Ray was Justice Of the Peace in 1890. On January 16, 1890, he solemnized the marriage rites between Daniel Long and Laura Hickam at the home of Isaac Hickam.

The Gilead trustees at the time of the new building construction were Nathaniel Cotton and S. B. Moberly. The Rev. A. J. Pike was pastor during the building of the new church. He was pastor from 1890 to 1905. Rev. Pike must have taken a leave of absence for about a year because the records show L. P. Johnson as pastor in 1898. Pike returned to Gilead from 1912 to 1915. My grandfather, Les Long, was baptized and became a member of Gilead in 1914. Family members have quoted Les as saying, "Pike was the best pastor Gilead ever had". He was baptized in Silver Creek at the Iron Bridge at Barnes Mill. This was a popular body of water for baptisms during this time.

Other locations used over the years by not only Gilead, but other local congregations were: the Cunnius hole, a large body of water in Silver Creek, and Joe Long's pond at Round Hill. The Cunnius hole was named for Jacob Cunnius, who lived nearby. The 1860 Madison County census shows Jacob Cunnius to be 94 years old. His place of birth was Pennsylvania. Joe Long's farm pond at Round Hill was a popular location in the 1930's. Many of my own people were baptized here, including my parents and various aunts and uncles.

These Baptismal services, which were usually held on Sunday afternoons, were very well attended. The banks of the creeks or ponds were lined with people. There are several old record books at Gilead dating back many years. In some of the ledgers it is interesting that male and female members are recorded separately. In the May, 1895 female record, the names of Martha King and Dovie King Hill appear. This may be of some interest to the Long family since Martha was the sister of Daniel Long and Dovie was Martha's daughter. Dovie was married to Tom Hill. Another ledger records a business meeting held October 3, 1895. The following were presented as candidates for baptism: Emma Sowers, Pearl Snyder (Taylor), Nannie Tussy (Curtis), Henley Long, Perry Long and Matt Tussy.

It is not clear, nor is it that important when Bible study, or Sunday School began at Gilead. The earliest record found is dated 1887 showing J. W. Tudor as superintendent with a total of 20 scholars. All of us who hold Gilead dear owe a debt of gratitude to Ethel Turner Cates. Mrs. Cates has written a brief history of Gilead on the inside cover of one of the record books. This will be invaluable information for future generations at Gilead.

Members of my family have been a part of Gilead for well over a century. Jacob Moberly, the brother of my great, great grandmother, Elizabeth Moberly Long, was a trustee in 1877. My grandfather, Leslie Long, became a member in 1914. His father and mother, Daniel and Laura Long, did not become members until 1920. My grandmother, Annie Long, joined in 1917. My maternal grandparents, Denny and Fannie Anglin, by letter in 1933. My mother, Ruby Anglin Long, in 1928 and my father, James Long in 1933.

In rural Madison County, such as the Poosey Ridge area, the church was the hub of the community. Although no one would dare call it such, it was the local social center. Before the advent of the automobile, radio, television etc., the church was probably the major social center. People did not get to town too often and other than the few country stores and neighbor visiting neighbor, the church was just about the only other place to socialize. Although they would be quick to tell you they were there for the sole purpose of receiving spiritual food, they did not pass up the opportunity to catch up on the latest news in the area.

The revival meetings were the highlight of the year. They were usually held for a period of two weeks, sometimes longer. A guest evangelist was usually called, but sometimes the pastor would conduct the meetings. These meetings were very well attended. Scores of people would converge on the church from the hills, hollows and ridges much to the delight of the evangelist. Gilead was a rather large building for a rural church, and revival time would see it packed. What is almost inconceivable today is there were almost as many people in the yard outside as there were on the inside.

One would like to believe this enormous crowd on the outside was there because the inside was filled to capacity. The truth is there were men, young and old, who came every night for two weeks with no intention of going inside. Let me add that those who remained outside were male, rather than female. This group consisted of fellows from mid to late teens and up. Since these meetings were held during the summer, it was more pleasant for some to sit outside on the grass in the cool night air. While outside, some could smoke or chew and talk quietly among themselves.

As with most gatherings such as this, there was some mischief to be found and usually, it was nothing too serious. Even as late as the early to mid 1940's, there were still some people who rode horses to church. One popular prank among the young men was to turn the saddles around. It was usually very dark when services were over, and it was a surprise to find that one's saddle just didn't seem to sit like it should.

Revivals for these rural churches were very special events. They were events looked forward to from one year to the next. People, who never darkened the church door any other time, would never miss an evening service for the two-week duration. It was also common to have a morning service each day. Farmers would leave their fields wearing their work clothes, and women would leave their household chores arriving at the church about 10:00 a.m.. After about an hour of singing, praying and preaching, the congregation was dismissed to return to their daily routine.

As mentioned, these services were usually held during the summer. Folks would start gathering early in the hope of finding a seat near an open window. The warm weather combined with the crowded conditions and fiery sermons from the evangelist caused the temperature to be somewhat uncomfortable. Because the sermons were long and there were no nurseries, the preacher had to make himself heard above the sound of crying children who had become restless.

Several decisions could always be expected at this time. They included initial acts of faith, re-commitments, or coming by statement or letter from another church. If a decision was to be made, it seems people always wanted to wait for the revival to do it. People looked forward to revivals with great expectation. They were times of excitement and times of celebration. Many were sorry when they were over and experienced a sense of loss.

Another well-attended church function was the annual associational meeting. The Tates Creek Association of Baptists would (and still do) hold their meetings at a different church each year. These gatherings were usually two-day affairs in years past. The first day would be an all- day meeting with dinner on the grounds, as it was commonly referred to. Dinner was the term given to the noon meal. It was a feast prepared by the women of the host church. The event was held in the summer when fried chicken and fresh garden vegetables were in abundance. The fact that these meetings were held during the week did not discourage attendance. Men and women alike did not seem to mind interrupting their normal routines in order to attend.

There was much business on the agenda and rules of decorum were followed closely. Moderators, clerks, etc., had been elected in advance. The same was true of the messengers, who were elected by their various congregations to report on the progress of their respective churches the preceding year. And as one might guess, a rousing sermon or two would probably be heard before it was over. The following information is taken from the minutes of an associational meeting held at Gilead August 23 and 24, 1939:

Moderator: Rev. W. P. Rogers
Assistant Moderator: Rev. W. R. Royce
Secretary of Executive Board: E. R. Prather
Clerk: John Caldwell
Assistant Clerk: G. L. Borders
Chairman of Executive Board: R. Don Gambrell
Gilead Messengers: Leslie Long, Charlie Isaac, Ollie Casey and Mrs. O. E. Click
The report showed W. R. Royce as pastor of Gilead and also being pastor of Calvary in Richmond at the same time.
Church Clerk: Mrs. O. E. Click
Sunday School Superintendent: Harry Sebastian

There were certain unwritten laws churches seemed to abide by. One of these laws, especially at a rural church like Gilead, dictated that the preacher was to have the Sunday noon meal with one of the church families. Families took turns in providing this meal. There never seemed to be any controversy as to who would assume this duty because it was a tradition. There was no problem in determining whose home the preacher was going to on a given Sunday, because the lady of the house would not attend the morning service. Every one knew she was home, in the kitchen, preparing a banquet.

When the preacher arrived at the host's home, he would be greeted by the lady. She would instruct him not to look at the dirty house and in the same breath apologize for the lack of food available for his consumption. The truth was the table was literally sagging beneath the abundance of food. It was meals such as these that gave rise to the rumor regarding Baptist preachers' enormous capacity for fried chicken. With the exception of the good food, this was not a happy time for the children of the family—especially the boys. They were expected to keep their Sunday clothes on all afternoon and be on their best behavior.

My earliest memory of Gilead pastors goes back to W. R. Royce. Royce was Gilead's pastor from 1935 to 1939 and again for a short time in 1945. When my family left Dry Branch in late 1943, we attended the Peytontown Baptist Church where he was pastor. Royce was very proud of his Irish ancestry and said he got his temper and his sense of humor from his Irish mother, Elvira O'Hargett. My dad, Jim Long, told Royce a story about a hunting dog. Dad said whenever he made a hide tanning board, he had a dog that would then proceed to catch an animal the correct size to fit the board. One day he was making my mother an ironing board, the dog left and never returned. As long as the two men lived, whenever they met, the first question Royce would ask my father was "Jim, did you ever find your dog?"

Royce did not enter the ministry until he was 36 years of age. Although he started rather late in life, he was an ordained minister for 60 years. I was baptized by W. R. Royce in the summer of 1947. Some of the families who attended Glead, as I remember them, are as follows: Charlie Isaac, Ollie Casey, George Prather, Ballard

Scrivener, O. E. Click, Sam Long, Harry Sebastian, Bourbon Turner, Burdette Agee, Simp Rogers, James Rhodus, Luther Proctor, Lewis Ward, Willie Carl Prather, Ollie Prewitt, Russell Ross, Charlie B. Agee and the Taylors.

The above list of names in no way represents all the families who attended Gilead during the period my family was part of this church. The time period I am referring to is now at least 60 years ago, and some names and faces have eluded my memory.

I have in my possession an item which I can refer to that will remind me of many of the people who lived in this area at that time. In the late 1930's a group of Gilead ladies came up with a money-making idea they thought would benefit the church. They decided to make a quilt with names embroidered in small blocks. For ten cents per name one could have as many names on the quilt as was desired. There are 480 names on the quilt. They decided to auction the quilt to the highest bidder. For some reason they did not think it proper to auction it off on church property, so they went next door and had the auction in George Prather's front yard. My mother, Ruby Long, purchased the quilt for the sum of $3.50. She gave it to me in the late 1950's and it has become one of my most prized heirlooms.

Gilead began to have its annual home coming events in 1982. It was my privilege to be able to attend the first one and several successive ones. It was a joy for me to be able to renew old relationships as well as establish new ones. One of the first things I noticed when entering the sanctuary was its pews were the same ones they had when I was a child. My grandmother, Annie Long, who was born in 1895, told me she began attending Gilead in 1911 after she married my grandfather. In her opinion, the pews that were being used in 1982 were the original pews placed there in 1892 when the church was built. The old pews eventually were replaced with new ones in the late 1980's.

The REA (rural electric) came to Poosey Ridge in 1939 and I assume Gilead was wired for electricity shortly afterwards. I do, however, remember the kerosene wall lamps with their reflectors and the circle of lamps suspended from the ceiling. George Prather, who lived next door to the church, was the custodian. When the evening services were over, George would immediately start fanning out the lamps with his hat.

As was mentioned, my family has been a part of Gilead for well over a century. This church has a special meaning for me as it did my father before me. The point of this writing was not to produce a history of Gilead for the sake of history only, but that my children and grandchildren may in some way become a part of its heritage as I feel I am.

Poosey Methodist Church

In the Poosey Ridge area, church denominational groups were limited primarily to the Baptist and Christian churches. This situation had remained constant since around 1830. All of this changed in the very early 1940's when two young Methodist ministers by the name of Elijah Thornton "E. T." Perkins and Roland Brooks came to Poosey for the purpose of holding a tent revival. The tent was pitched on the property of Mr. Elbert Chandler. I do not recall whether it was a one or two week affair, but I do recall it was very well attended and generated much excitement.

The tent was wired for electricity and there was sawdust to walk on. I had never been in a tent before and it was all very exciting to me. As with the local church revivals, people converged on the tent in scores. They came from the hills and hollows by car, by horseback and on foot. Our family lived on Turner's Ridge at this time and I remember walking the entire distance. We walked down the hill, crossed Dry Branch, up the hill past where Roy Taylor lived, came out on Poosey Ridge road near Miss Emma Sowers' store and walked down the road to the meeting. As we walked along we would be joined by other pedestrians headed for the same destination.

As with the local revivals, there seemed to be almost as many people outside as inside. This revival was so successful that many embraced the Methodist faith to the point seeds were sown which eventually blossomed into the Poosey Methodist Church. This is not to say some did not already have a Methodist background, but this tent revival added fuel to the fire. When this series of meetings was over, there were several of the good folk who were convinced the Poosey area was definitely in need of a Methodist church.

There were members of my own family who were part of this original assembly. Among the pioneers of this new work were my aunt and uncle, Luther and Mary Laura Proctor, as well as members of the following families: Hendren, Davis and Goodlett. I am sure there were other families equally active. How to get organized and where were meetings to be held until a building could be completed were the pressing questions. In order to generate interest in this new group, cottage prayer meetings were held in various homes in the community.

Jess Davis seemed to be the most visible in conducting these meetings. Jess was the son of Irvin and Nora Warren Davis. Nora herself was a very active member of this assembly. Jess's brother, Les, and his wife, Jenny Belle, also were active members. Even though my own family members were dyed in the wool Baptists, they did agree to host one of these cottage prayer meetings when we lived on Turner's Ridge. Jess was the leader, and as I recall, it was well attended. Still, my father and mother had no intention of becoming affiliated with this newly formed group. Out of respect for Jess and the other members my father had known all of his life, he and my mother were more than happy to open our home to them.

An arrangement was made with the Poosey School allowing the new body to have Sunday services in its building. Mary Laura Proctor said that as far as she knew, they continued to have services there until the new building was finished. I personally was privileged to attend at least one of the services, maybe more, at the school in the very early 1940's. In attendance were those one would expect to see, such as the Hendren, Davis, Goodlett and Proctor families. After all, they were the founding families of this new work.

There was one who attended faithfully whom I recall. Uncle Bud Sallee was an elderly distinguished looking gentleman, who rode horseback when weather permitted. According to one source who was contacted, Uncle Bud was never an official member, but was usually counted among the faithful in attendance. It is believed since Uncle Bud had raised his family on Silver Creek, he might have been a member of the old Friendship Church. At the time he was attending the Methodist church, he supposedly was living on Sled Branch. He rode a rather large bay horse with four white stockings or socks. It is said one could hear him coming because he sang as he rode.

Another willing participant in this new endeavor was Robert Oliver. Uncle Robert, as he was called by the members of my family, was married to Jenny Long Oliver. Jenny was the sister of my grandfather, Les Long. From the church's early beginning, Robert took an active role even though he was a member of Salem Christian Church.

There are two ladies deserving of mention because of their faithfulness and dedication to this body of believers. They are Hattie Lee Hendren and Nora Davis. I am sure for the period of time this body has been in existence, there have been many women totally devoted to this church. I choose to single out these two women because I personally remember them. I also have heard members of my family praise them for their efforts. One long time member said these two women emerged as pillars of the church in the early days. As I write this I am reminded of a statement my father has made over the years. He said he loved to be in the congregation during a song service and hear Nora Davis sing "The Pearly White City".

As the church continued to meet in the Poosey School House, plans were being made for a new building. A piece of property owned by Mr. Perry Warren, a relative of Nora Davis, was chosen for the location of the new edifice. Arrangements were made to purchase the property. Four men who agreed to sign for the purchase: Harold Hendren, Luther Proctor, Jess Davis and George Goodlett. As best as can be determined, the men of the church supplied the labor for the most part. I have been told that Robert Oliver, who was quite a craftsman in his own right, did much of the work. Also, Bill Cates hauled much of the lumber for the construction.

I had some difficulty determining exactly what year the building was completed. I believe it was June of 1990 when I arrived at the church around noon on Sunday to find Mr. Obra Collins and Pastor Ted Beam getting ready to depart. It was my good fortune to be able to talk to these two men for a while. Mr. Collins, a long time member and a very pleasing gentleman, said the building was completed in 1955. I have a photograph with a very large display of II Chronicles 7:14 on the front lawn of the church. In the photo, Mr. Collins and the Rev. Beam are standing on each end of the display.

Even though I have not been even remotely involved with the Poosey Methodist Church for approximately 60 years at the time of this writing, I still feel a kinship with this faithful body. After all, I was present at the dawning of its existence. Compared to Salem or Gilead, this congregation is a relative newcomer to the area from a longevity standpoint. Regardless as to the length of time this church has been active, it would be difficult indeed to measure the impact it has had on the community as well as what it has meant to many families throughout the years. The good folk, who were responsible for the forming and nurturing of this body, would be pleased (and perhaps they are) to discover their dream is still very much alive.

Salem Christian Church

Like Gilead, the Salem Christian Church has been part of the Poosey community almost from the time the area was settled. Salem, which in its very early existence was known as Bear Wallow, was organized and constituted as a Baptist church around 1808. It continued as a Baptist fellowship until around 1830. At that time the influence of Alexander Campbell and Barton W. Stone caused many Baptist churches in Madison County to embrace a new reformation which became known as the Disciples or Christian church.

When Forest Calico wrote the history of Salem in his remarkable book "A Story Of Four Churches", the new church had not been built. The church he wrote about was built in 1867. He said there had been two or perhaps three buildings up to that time. The old log structure that preceded the 1867 building was destroyed by fire sometime prior to the Civil War.

It seems as if all buildings were built on their original locations. For example, the church that was built in 1867 was erected on the same spot as the old log building earlier destroyed by fire. In like manner, the 1867 building was razed in 1952 to make room for the new structure, which was dedicated in June of 1953. The new Salem church is an elegant brick edifice. I am sure the church members as well as the community are very proud of it.

As was mentioned earlier, when I lived in the area, Salem and Gilead were the only two church buildings on Poosey Ridge. There always seemed to be a sense of cooperation between these two churches. It was quite common for members of the Gilead Church to move their membership to Salem and vice versa. Many of the Gilead congregation would attend the Salem revivals as many of Salem did Gilead's. This shared attitude between the two fellowships could be due to the fact they both sprang from the same roots.

I appreciate the fact I have in my file a photograph of the old Salem building which was taken around 1950 as plans were already being made to replace it with the new building. It has been my pleasure to have known personally some long time members of Salem. In the mid 1980's I was able to renew my acquaintance with Mr. Stratton Stocker. He shared with me some information about his father, Ellie, which appears in another section of this writing. C. W. and Neal Burnham Whittaker, father and son, were a very important part of my childhood as I visited Whittaker's Store. Burdette Land is also remembered by me because my father worked for him during a brief period in the late 1940's and early 1950's.
The following are excerpts taken from the program of dedication of the new building dated June 7, 1953:

Pastor.........................Joseph L. Bryan
Present officers and teachers
Chairman of Board............ Mr. Ernest Collins
Secretary......................Mr. Neal B. Whittaker
Treasurer......................Mr. Russell Whitaker
Sunday School Superintendent Mr. Stratton Stocker

Teachers
Men's Class...Mr. Clayton Reynolds, Mr. Neal B. Wittaker
Women's Class.................Mrs. C. C. Burton
Junior Class.................... Mrs. Ernest Collins
Primary Class................. Miss Shelby Stocker, Rev. Joe L. Bryan
Ladies Aid President.........Mrs. Tommy Cotton

Building Committee

Mr. Shirley Land
Mr. C. W. Whittaker
Mr. Stratton Stocker
Mr. Ernest Collins
Mr. Burdette Land

Contractor

Mr. Burdette Land

Presentation of Pulpit Bible

Judge Forest Calico

Former Pastors

Rev. E. C. Cosby
Rev. Elmer Ray
Rev. Dick Spangler
Rev. June Fraklin Dennis*

*From September 1948 to March 1950 I attended the Waco Community School. This was probably June Franklin Dennis' junior and senior years in high school. I remember him very well and it was clear he had already embarked upon the path of Christian service. In those days the Friday convocation was still referred to as chapel and June Franklin was called upon from time to time to lead the assembly in prayer. As I end this tribute to Salem, I could not end with a more fitting benediction than what was written on the back of the program of dedication for that June 7, 1953 event:

"THE FUTURE

Salem Christian Church stands dedicated to the future as it has been consecrated in the past. This new building is not the final expression in our stewardship of giving. Rather it is indicative of things to come. We, who are its members, are full of faith and hope for the future. We know that with God's love, working in and through us, all things are possible. It is our fervent prayer that he will continue to bless us, enrich us, guide us, and at last save us, in the name of His Son, our Lord and Savior, Jesus Christ".

Salem Christian Church
Built in 1867, razed in 1952 to provide room for the new building

Rev. John G. Pond

Chapter Twenty Five

Schools Of Poosey Ridge

In every locale, the schools as well as the churches are and have always been an all important element of the life of the community. This fact was no less true in the Poosey Ridge area. There were several schools that were active at one time or another at various locations on the ridge. There were only two active schools I can personally remember, the Cottonburg and Poosey schools. Although this school was no longer in operation, I recall the building next to Miss Emma Sowers' store where the Hendren School was located. I am going to attempt to identify some of these educational institutions that were and are no more. I am sure since this area was settled in the 1790's there have been many such schools which have come and gone that are no longer part of anyone's memory. However, thankfully there are those among us who can still remember or have first hand knowledge of these old schools.

I will begin with the Cottonburg School in the upper part of the ridge road and proceed on down the ridge toward the river. The Cottonburg School has been mentioned previously in this writting, but I will elaborate in more detail. As pointed out earlier, many of my own family attended this old school. It was my good fortune several years ago to come into possession of small individual photographs of the 1938 class of Cottonburg, including the teacher, Ophelia Estes. I think it is important that these students be listed by name. They are as follows:

Cecil Baker	Ernest Baker	Linda Broadus	Ralph Carpenter
Joe Estes	Ray Hamm	Buddy Humes	Clyde Long
Louise Long	Roberta Long	Burnam Miller	Vernon Prather
Kyle Prewitt	Harold Rogers	Royce Rogers	Frank Taylor
Mildred Whittaker			

Cottonburg School was located next to the Owen Click Store. Mary Laura Long Proctor said she had received information that the property the building was on was donated by members of the Schooler family. This school building was converted to a residence soon after the 1938 class. I do not recall ever being in the building while it was a school, but I was there a few times after it became the home of Mr. and Mrs. Bill Pollard and their daughter, Vilvia. There had never been any activity in the building known as the Hendren School during the time I lived in that area. However my father did attend that school for a while.

The largest school building in the area was the Poosey School. I have a photograph taken approximately 1922 of the original building with the student body gathered together in front with the teachers. My aunt, Lula Witt Anglin, my father, James "Jim" Long, and his brother, Vernon, are in the picture. The teachers at that time were Harriet Million and Creighton "C. W." Whittaker. Above the entrance are the words Poosey Consolidated School.

Unfortunately, and to the dismay of the community and most of the students, this building burned December 16, 1932. Thankfully, and to the delight of many I am sure, the replacement was constructed in 1933. It has been said that while the new building was being built, the students attended school at Cottonburg. When further consolidation of the county schools became necessary and the old building was no longer needed as a school, it became a residence. I would like to thank Neal B. Whittaker for providing the dates of the school's destruction by fire and its reconstruction.

There are three more old schools deserving of mention: Sallee, Wylie and Burton. Again I would like to give special recognition to my friend of many years, Neal B. Whittaker, for providing information relating to these old schools as well as adding some individual information about his parents, Creighton "C. W" and Mabel Whittaker. I will take the liberty of referencing a few paragraphs from a letter received from Neal B. dated October 22, 2002. In Neal's own words..."The Sallee School was the first one my father taught. Somebody bought the farm then pushed the school into the hollow or ravine. My father rode a horse from Granny Whitaker's home then the calves at night chewed its tail off. My mother, Mabel Teater was his pupil, then on June 15, 1917 he married her."

"Nearby was the Wylie School on the New Road just south of the Sallee School. This place was called "Stand Around". My mother went to Wylie School when she was about ten years old. This would have been about 1910. The Burton School was located where Luther Reynolds ran a store, grist mill and black smith shop under the same roof. This school was located 1/2 mile south of Salem Christian Church at the Bogie Lane and Poosey Ridge Road".

Thank you, Neal B., for sharing your memories of these old, but not altogether forgotten schools.

Chapter Twenty Six

Branches

The Poosey Ridge topography for the most part consists of ridges, hollows and roads which follow the tributaries leading to either Silver or Paint Lick creeks. These roads that follow the tributaries are referred to as branch roads, or simply branches. The branches will be the focus of this account of the area known a Poosey Ridge. As this area began to be settled in the 1790's, it did not take long for the hills and hollows to become well populated. I can affirm as a native of this area, that I have lived on a ridge (Turners) and two branches (Moberly and Dry).

I will attempt to begin at what most people regard as the beginning of Poosey Ridge Road and name as many of the branch roads as I can along with some of the people who lived on them at the time my family lived in this area. Drawing near to where road #595 makes a sharp left turn at Page Hill Road (also road #876), there is a road that exits off to the left known as Gilead Branch. Some of the good folk who lived here many years ago were the following families: Charlie Warmouth, Jesse Baker, William King and Jesse Prewitt. The next road to the right just beyond the Gilead Cemetery was Moberly Branch. This has already been covered in detail earlier as has Dry Branch.

The next road to the right leading down to Silver Creek was known as Trace Branch. Local legend says its name was derived from the fact it was first called Boone's Trace, because Daniel Boone would travel this route on his way from Boonesboro to Stanford. I have always derived a certain pleasure from the thought I could have walked on the same ground as Daniel Boone. I have been told there were only two houses on this branch. Some of the families that resided there from time to time were those of Major Ham, Luther Proctor and Floyd King.

The Kelly or Marg Turner Branch was accessed almost directly across the ridge road from the entrance to Trace Branch. Whereas most of the streams that formed what became known as branch roads flowed to either Silver or Paint Lick Creeks, this stream wound its way to Dry Branch, which was one of the tributaries of Paint Lick Creek. The Les Long family lived on this branch at one time. Their daughter, Mary Laura, was born here in 1917. The Ollie Casey family lived at the intersection of Kelly and Dry Branches.

The next branch road to exit off of the ridge road is that of Duck Branch. Some families who are remembered as living here are Merrit Long, Jeff Long and Willie Curtis. Quoting directly from Calico's "A Story of Four Churches", "The Wheeler Branch Road has had four mouths that I have known". I personally have no information with respect to this, however, Mr. Calico grew up in this area and I certainly would never question his considerable knowledge on this subject. Some families who lived on this branch at one time or another were Jess Land, Jasper May, Vernon Long and Dick Hall.

Again quoting from Calico, "The Pilate or Pilant Branch was named for a man named Pilant who lived at the creek called Paint Lick. He was a brother-in-law to "Old Dave Vincent" a veteran of the War of 1812, our second war with Great Britain. This branch is now called Sled Branch." I am once again obliged to Mr. Calico for his willingness to provide some most valuable historical data pertinent to this area. In my lifetime I have never heard it referred to by any name other than Sled Branch. His reference to the War of 1812 might give one an idea as to how long ago it was called Pilant Branch. Certain individuals who lived on this branch road were Fount Whitaker, Fletch Teater, Gladys Ward and Vernon Long. Vernon's son, Marvin, was born while he lived here.

There are two other roads that may or may not qualify as branch roads. These are Stone House Hill and Reagan Lane. Both of these roads proceed in the direction of Silver Creek. Stone House Hill was named for the stone house built by John Ham around 1820 at the foot of the hill near Silver Creek. This area of the creek was also known as Ham's Ford. In May of 1982, my aunt, Roberta Long Evans

129

and I were exploring this area. As I was riding with her in her Ford pick-up truck, she cautiously made her way down Stone House Hill. We went past the old stone house, which by this time was in ruins, and drove across Silver Creek at Ham's Ford. I guess one could say we drove the Ford across the Ford.

After living in Indiana for many years where most of the creeks have sand and gravel bottoms, I was amazed to see a creek bed that looked like it had been paved with concrete from bank to bank. The enormous slab of what I determined to be limestone expanded as has been referred to, from bank to bank and for some distance up and down the creek. The centuries of water continually flowing over this gigantic section had brought about a remarkably smooth surface over which to drive. There was about a foot of water in the creek at the time and we proceeded across with no difficulty.

Reagen Lane was named, no doubt for Robert Reagen, who ran a store and post office at Edenton. As Bert, as I called my aunt, and I crossed Silver Creek, I was reminded we were not that far from the small community of Newby. This realization brought back a memory that in itself was connected to Poosey Ridge.

Chapter Twenty Seven

Old Golden, Page Hill

When our family lived on Lancaster Pike in the mid 1940's, I had a burning desire to have a horse of my own. My dad, who had been open to this reverie of mine, mentioned that very soon we would drive over to Newby and take a look at one of Old Golden's colts. I was very familiar with the name, "Old Golden", since I had heard my father talk of him many times, but I had never seen him. This horse was owned by the Hendren's, a Poosey Ridge family known for its excellent saddle horses. Old Golden had established the reputation as one of the most prolific sires in that part of the county. The very few people I have interviewed who still remember this stallion all agree he was a descendant of Rex Peavine, which has been referred to in an earlier segment of this narrative.

My grandfather, Les Long, began working for Newt Hendren on the farm when he was a mere youth and continued off and on until manhood. As I recall, Newt had three sons, Oscar, Harold and Earl. I have never heard Mr. Hendren referred to by any name other than Newt, but I assume his name was Newton. One thing I do personally remember about the Hendren's livestock is a spotted jack. This was a bit unusual. I have no idea if he ever produced any spotted mules. If he did, none was brought to my attention.

My dad and I did travel to Newby to look at Old Golden's colt. Because Dad used the term "colt", I expected to see just that! I was surprised to learn the colt turned out to be an aged gelding. I do not recall the details, but the purchase never materialized. I was very disappointed even though my dream colt was actuality what I would consider to be an old horse.

It has always been of interest to me how various locations such as roads, ridges, branches etc. happen to come by their names. It is obvious to those of us who have been familiar to the area for years how some of these names might have occurred. The sources of many of the other names have been lost in the indistinct mists of time.

If you are traveling on road 595 in the direction of Poosey Ridge, you will eventually arrive at the intersection of 595 and 876. If you turn right on 876, this road will lead to somewhat of a steep incline before reaching Silver Creek. This for many years has been known as Page Hill. I wonder how many natives of that area are aware of how Page Hill was named. I have interviewed a few local residents and asked this question, but no one had any knowledge where the name came from. I'm sure there are a few people around who still remember the tale about the origin of Page Hill's name. Among them are my aunt Mary Laura Proctor, who was born in 1917.

I have heard this story from my youth. It was told to me by my father. My father had heard it from his grandfather, Dan Long, who personally knew Page Smith. The following is a brief account of Page Smith: A black man, who lived in the Silver Creek area, Mr. Smith had a strange request as to where his final resting place should be. His request was to be buried in the section of land on the left going down hill that lies between the road and the stream which flows into Silver Creek. According to older residents, his grave is located just about half way down the hill, so it became known as "Page Hill". I never travel Page Hill Road without being reminded of that long ago incident. Page Smith is listed in the 1880 Kirksville precinct census along with his wife, children and two nephews. His age is shown as 40, which would have made him 16 years older than my great grandfather at the time they knew each other.

Chapter Twenty Eight

The Hills That Beckon

I lived the first almost 9-1/2 years of my life in this area. Although I was quite young when my family left the area in late 1943, I believe family, friends and the land had already made an impression on me. Each time I am privileged to visit the region, I marvel at just how steep those hills are. For those who are not familiar with this area, they are hills, not mountains. I am reminded of a conversation I had with Frank Taylor several years ago. Even though the hills are very steep, they are for the most part free of trees and underbrush and are mowed to resemble an English countryside. I asked Frank what was used to mow these steep hills and he replied, "A tractor". When I voiced some surprise that a tractor could remain upright on those slopes, he said "sure we use a tractor. Why there ain't a mule in this country".

In 1950 my family and I moved from Madison County to Columbus, Indiana. Columbus has the distinct honor of being referred to as the "Athens of the Prairie" because of its impressive architecture. Each time I visit Poosey Ridge I am reminded of a line from the Fox/Calhoun song, "The Hills Of Home". The line I'm referring to is: "My prairie home is beautiful but oh, I miss the broken skyline that I know".

No matter where I am or how long I am away, the hills of home continue to call me back. As I look back over the years to when I first launched this project, I am reminded of the many people, family and acquaintances, who contributed to its content. I regret it has taken so long to complete this work since I solicited help and information from so many family members and friends who are no longer with us. So many of the stories and narratives found within this volume have been familiar to me from the time of my youth.

My father, Jim Long, never seemed to tire of telling these stories over and over and I never became weary of hearing them. His

133

grandfather, Daniel Long, was quite a story teller himself and much of the information came from him through his grandson, Jim. It seems that after my father left this area, the old familiar stories became a link between him, Poosey Ridge, Moberly Branch, etc. In a manner of speaking, they also became my link because for some reason that small section of geography in northwest Madison County became more endearing to me as the years wore on.

My father died in February of 1981, and I realized that my major link with what he referred to as "down home" was gone. I miss many things concerning my father. I obviously miss his presence most of all, but I also regret the fact I no longer hear those old familiar tales relating to family and people, in general, regarding Poosey Ridge and the neighboring locale. Not only did I experience a great sense of loss with the death of my father, but also an almost unexplained feeling of longing to reconnect with that area and the few remaining people that I knew. I still had aunts, uncles and cousins living in Madison County, but there was no one living in the Poosey area any longer with the exception of my great uncle, Sam Long. He died July 26, 1982 at the age of 82.

Over the years I had visited my relatives from time to time, but never seemed to make it to Poosey. Several months after my father's death, I began to experience a gnawing sensation that I should in some manner document those stories. After all, I was an only child and if I didn't do it, who would? I began to carry a small notebook in my shirt pocket and any time I thought of something I considered worth remembering, I would write it down. What to do with this data was the question. I began to toy with the idea of organizing this information into some type of manageable formulation such as a book. Then I asked myself the question: how? I was not an author nor had I ever written anything worthy of print.

Despite the fact I felt desperately unqualified, I began to feel it was my duty to at least do something to perpetuate these family narratives for the sake of my children, grandchildren and perhaps even for future generations. When I had resolved that some type of book was the best way to preserve this record, I consulted my good friend, Kenneth Murphy. Ken was head of the English department at Columbus East High School in Columbus and I shared my dilemma with him. I will never forget his wise counsel when he said, "the most difficult job you are going to have is getting the pen to move". I wish I could tell him just how right he was.

In September of 1982 the Gilead Baptist Church began their annul home comings. I began to attend these on a somewhat regular basis. As a result of these events I was able to renew old acquaintances and relationships with people I had not seen in years. I was also able to become familiar once again with the panorama, the hills, hollows and ridges that are so identifiably Poosey Ridge.

At the risk of sounding loquacious, let me once again emphasize that the objective of this writing was not for the benefit of those folks who are found within these pages, but for my children, grandchildren and hopefully unfolding generations. It is also my wish that family members of others who are referred to might be able to derive pleasure from what has been written concerning their relatives. It is my hope that this feeble attempt will help my family members to somehow better understand their heritage. Hopefully, this book will allow them to better appreciate their branch of the Longs for over a 200 year period. I only hope that, like me from time to time, they will not fail to respond to "The Hills That Beckon".